# salmonpoetry40

*Publishing Irish & International*
*Poetry Since 1981*

the arts council
an chomhairle ealaíon
funding literature
artscouncil.ie

# Light Rolling Slowly Backwards

## New & Selected Poems

# ETHNA McKIERNAN

Published in 2021 by
Salmon Poetry
Cliffs of Moher, County Clare, Ireland
Website: www.salmonpoetry.com
Email: info@salmonpoetry.com

ISBN 978-1-912561-95-7

Cover Photography: *Jessie Lendennie*
Cover Design & Typesetting: *Siobhán Hutson*

Printed in Ireland by Sprint Print

*For their help towards the production costs of this book, we wish to thank
Thomas Dillon Redshaw, Thomas Murtha & Stefanie Ann Lenway*

*I dedicate this book to the hundreds of homeless clients I've worked with through the years—to their resilience, courage and care for each other. This book is dedicated especially to Farid S., who wrote poems through his homelessness and told me once "the highway was his king-sized bed." Long may you live, Farid, and I pray you have housing now.*

# Contents

from *Caravan* (1989)

from *The One Who Swears You Can't Start Over* (2002)

from *Sky Thick With Fireflies* (2011)

from *Swimming With Shadows* (2019)

# Light Takes the Tree: New Poems

*"Of those so close beside me, which are you?*
*God bless the Ground! I shall walk softly there,*
*And learn by going where I have to go."*

Theodore Roethke

# Light

Light. The rapture of it, heft
and weight. Two birches wear the white sheen
of it, a zinnia's face blazes gold in it,
sidewalk shadows change size because of it.

Quick as that, a gloss of light lands
on the cricket's back, then leaves. Leaves in Fall
are charged with it, fierce light pulsing out
from colors against black bark after rain.

When dark falls, there is an absence,
a quiet sorrow in the realm of eyesight.
Edges blur and soften, and we no longer
recognize what we knew so keenly yesterday.

Then daybreak, when the rapt world flames forth
again, scattering bits of light, delirious light.

# Kintsugi, the Art of Precious Scars

*The wound is where the light enters—*

Rumi

That cracked      and mended bowl
     sealed with gold     bits of light and sparkle
at the crooked seam of pottery

recreates unbrokenness,     makes dazzle speak
     again,  makes forgiveness be the family
it should always be.

That handmade teapot missing
     a few flecks of glaze
on its sides?  Close your eyes.  Watch it glow.

I want the shaggy, nicked scratch,
     the coarse and jagged edge
that defies easy praise.

It's there we'll find the crack where light lives;
     there, where incandescence shines.

# Those Birds I Loved

*"Today there are three billion fewer birds than there were in 1970"*

—*The Atlantic*, 9-20-19

The bright yellow goldfinch
who turns brown in the winter
to match his mate is gone from the feeder;
the power lines are bare of starlings.

Brown swallows have been swallowed
into invisibility. Tiny hummingbirds,
their red whir and dart and hum
outside my window, all gone.

These mornings in spring I don't wake
to robins singing but to a startling quiet.
My red cardinals who cracked seeds
with their short thick bills are absent, too.

Bold noisy blue jays, the ones
with black necklaces and blue crests
have disappeared into the ether.
Mourning doves, their soft calls like an owl,

also gone.  Add them up
and they become the rainbow colors
of gasoline spilled in water—
crow, nuthatch, flicker, grackle, oh.

# Band-Aid

Snow fell lightly on the Greenway,
on the tents and tarps and bikes,
on the folding chairs
and barbeque stands, on
our backpacks heavy
with waters, hats and snacks,
on the cold trail of homelessness.

When Tracy couldn't stand
we propped her up in a chair,
the heroin too strong for our power
or hers. She laughed with her eyes
closed, nodding nodding down.
*Oh my God, do we need Narcan?*
someone asked but no, Tracy
jerked awake and then back out,
smiling her bliss and fucked-up pain
an alternating mile a minute.

We stayed till she was on her feet
and talking to the next guy,
promising she had a little bit
of something for him, silver earrings
flashing as she talked. Tracy love,
the last train is coming and I hope
you're not on it, hope like anything
you're still here tomorrow
on the Greenway in your tent,

hope the world opens soon
to a sweet crib for you, waltzes up
and zaps your homelessness forever.

Honey, hold on, hold on,
we have socks and gloves
and we'll be back tomorrow
with bus tokens
and another Band-Aid
for your sorrow.

# Oh, Maria

*One Thursday at Homeless Services*

More days than I'd like
I remember Maria staggering toward me
into the lobby and dying in my arms—
how I was wrong to think we needed to call Detox
rather than the ambulance, how she couldn't, except
with wild eyes, speak, but shook
and shook and shook.
The bright lights of the lobby
made me dizzy.
Maria slumped against me
and I yelled for water, water, someone get water,
but when I held the glass to her lips,
her fingers pushed mine away
and she began to choke.
I just didn't get how fast
she was slipping away, how
I should have yelled for more help
and put her on the floor to do CPR,
if I remembered, God help me, how.
No pulse, but I kept holding her.
I remember paramedics
coming in and in an instant Maria
was on the floor with her shirt up
and a defibrillator striking her chest
with one shock after another as her head
bounced back upon the pillow they'd placed
beneath her. They took her away
just as fast, hoping for a heartbeat.
Oh, Maria, how I laughed at your antics weekly,
how you kept your tent
so neat, how when I took you to get groceries
at Rainbow Foods with your food stamps,
we pushed the same grocery cart
as if we were sisters out for a stroll.

# Stigma, the Streets

*Stigma—from Greek and Latin words meaning*
*a mark on the skin, often coming from a hot iron*

Is stigma a scourge
and what is the weight of it?

Can it be scrubbed off, erased?

Do you have PTSD, have you ever
screamed in the night, are you fat
and someone cut you with their laugh,
did you hurt your brother
only to ride the long loneliness
in a cell? Was it ordinary,
the bullying of childhood?
Did you drink too much
and they said *hey! Don't worry!*

I remember how the saliva
pooled in my mouth, horrified, when
Jenny showed me the burn
from where they held her down
to place the hot iron
on her stomach,
and how she gave me her Oxy to hold
for safekeeping at the Outreach office
on Nicollet Curve.
I waited two days to open the bottle
and examine one, but my hands shook
and I dropped the pill back in.

Does generosity ever come without
judgment
or do the little hooks hold on
forever?

Who loves you, anyway?  Go to them
and plead forgiveness for a thing
you never wanted, never asked for.

Bow your head.
This, this is the weight.

# When She is Leaving

Liam talks about his wife's memory
lapses, how the kettle whistles an insistent
tune on the stove for the forgotten tea
and how lightning slices seize
her words and make them disappear
from her open lips. *Oh*, she says,
*I can't find anything*, batting the air
in front of her.

All the small losses make
a thousand deaths. The day she doesn't
recognize you for the first time,
the morning that she thinks you are
her sister, the evening in the bath
when she believes she is in bed
and wants the covers pulled up to her chin.

Daily she sheds old identities,
advanced degrees, the teaching years,
her skillful sewing of the children's clothes,
refrains from "I'll Be Seeing You"
and other velvet songs she hummed
around the house.
See how she grows smaller
by the minute, another version of herself.

Today the leaves blaze yellow
and maroon. Leaves, when she is gone,
cover her lovely face beneath you
and remember, please, who she was.

# Influenza 1918

My father was a three-year-old
when the doctors said
he wouldn't last the morning,
the engine of fever roaring
through his head,
his breathing a hot steam.
My grandmother had prayed
goodbye in that Manhattan hospital,
then left him in the hallway
crammed with other cots.

*In a single day in Philadelphia, 759 people died from flu-related illnesses.*

Sickness stomped and ambushed
each neighborhood,
every corner of the globe. So much
was unknown.

*Sept. 1918—1,543 soldiers at Camp Devens alone—*
*35 miles from Boston—were diagnosed with the flu in one day.*

One soldier coughed, and rows
of burial stones appeared
like upright dominos.
From Fort Riley the disease
spread east to battlefields
of Europe, the way the wind
takes seeds flung and scattered
from a woman's skirt as new growth
appears a continent away.

*The 1918 Influenza Pandemic left scars on nearly every part of the planet.*
*Fourteen percent of Fiji's population died in just 16 days. Entire villages*
*were wiped off the planet forever by the virus.*

Upstate from Manhattan,
maybe Syracuse,
a family is cleaning house.
When the child's parents
learned flu lurked in every part
of their daughter's room, they burned it all—
books, blankets,
the ballerina figurine above the jewelry box,
dresses, stuffed teddy bears,
even the lamp and rug in flames.
The lashes of the daughter's doll
blink as she crackles in the bonfire
below the big home.

*In October 1918 alone, 195,000 Americans died.*

My father lived.  His rich life
was an accident of fate, a slim kindness
carved from tragedy.  At 89
he joined the generation long gone
to the pandemic of the century,
the 1918 Spanish flu.

# In the Time of April 2020

On a walk under the sharp blue
sky, a little prayer of gratitude
along the wide-armed Mississippi—
*It could have been me,* I think,
on the ventilator at Mercy Hospital.

The sheer mystery, the randomness
of it all despite our best hand-washing,
sanitizers and the masks.  I just learned
the author of the masterpiece *Stones of Aran,*
Tim Robinson and his wife Máiréad
are both dead of the virus.  We visited
them in Roundstone, Conamara,
in the mid-90s, my father and I.
There is a picture on my bookshelf
of the four of us.

I'm looking for a song to sing
on my walk. "What a Wonderful World"
cheers me and then depresses me.
Coldplay's "Fix You" is closer,
or maybe "Sad-Eyed Lady of the Lowlands"
for its relentless melancholy.

Two miles ahead I turn
back, the sun on my shoulders
and none of the world's bright answers
jingling in my pockets.

# Jupiter Crosses Saturn

*December 22, 2020*

The year of pandemic, weariness and
fear. The year of no stars, of small hope,
of sky gone dark.
A year of pandemic, weariness and fear.
How many dead today, O Lord?

But when two planets
meet like this, whole centuries
between them, our world groans
with joy despite itself.
There is Jupiter, the star of miracles.
with Saturn, the God of change.

Every day the grass grows, a marvel
that we barely notice. Change careens
toward us and we follow its bewildered scent
to a forest like no other.
Longing is our new friend, and
the air sharpens
with it.

We still have the dead to bury
and to bury in chaos
and in grief we
recall the famous poet's words
*"Mere anarchy is loosed upon*
*the world"*
and we pray.

Stars and planets, constellations
of our human stories,
can you help us
as we nudge forward
to the light?

# The Day My Mother Gave Me Away
# to the Tinkers

She'd threatened this before, thinking
it would cause me great fear after
whatever I did the umpteenth time.
She with nine children that year in Dublin,
and me the boldest and the worst.

I couldn't wait to be among them,
their bright scarves and tools
and horse-drawn caravans,
their campfires at night and sounds
of fiddles and tin whistles, the mattress
with moonlight shining
on the three babies piled upon it.

Travelling was an itch, raw
and sweet in my bones.
How could I live on plain
Mount Auburn Avenue and walk
to Muckross School when
the world of mountains
and berries and lakes
awaited?

How could I carry that sliced loaf
of bread from Johnston Mooney and O'Brien's
when we could shape our own
and smell the yeast rising
from hot stones?

When I looked back,
my beautiful mother
was crying.  It would be a year
before I returned, changed.
How I'd miss her.

# Jessie's Basement, 1968

What I remember is the Rolling Stones
singing "Let's Spend the Night Together,"
and how longing rose in my throat
like a diesel engine, loud and hot
as my arms circled my boyfriend,
steam rising from us both;
how I wanted nothing more
at that moment.

Her parents were out. It was a party
of young teens, unleashed
and ripe. One couple danced themselves
into the bathroom and locked the door.
The huge basement was dark except
for strings of glittering Christmas lights
long past the season, and the music
throbbed through our veins the way
I imagined LSD might.

We thought we heard her father.
Maybe he let us carry on
a while longer before Elaine passed out
near the liquor cabinet
and I lost my hard-breathing boyfriend
to another girl in the dark.

I remember her Dad yelling as he bound
down the stairs while the whole romantic
hot evening of boys and booze and music
dissipated into the warm spring air,
Van Morrison's "Brown Eyed Girl" blasting
through the emptied basement door.

# Flying High

It was January 1986 and I was *en route*
to Dublin, six months pregnant with my first.
All the flights now banned smoking, and we
were held on the tarmac four hours
at JFK, waiting to take off.  I was large,
uncomfortable, and desperate for a smoke.

I wondered, though, how would they know
what went on in their locked toilets
when the fan was on?  Afterward, I'd lather up
some soap on the washcloth
and wand its sweetness through the air
before I walked the narrow aisle back to my seat.
Who would ever know.

Seconds after the match met my cigarette
the alarm screeched on, louder
and then louder still, as red lights flashed
overhead and a microphone droned
*this is a non-smoking plane.*

I was escorted to my seat, waves of shame
reddening my cheeks,
a scarlet S glowing from my chest,
the disapproving eyes of passengers
looking me up and down
as I seat-belted my large belly.

When the lights went out,
I crunched that Marlboro pack
to smithereens and sang the baby
all my twisted, blue *sorries*
across the whole dark Atlantic.

# Hey Diddle Diddle

Remember how it was then,
the desperate scratch and search
for babysitters who didn't leave
condoms behind the couch?
How did we do it in those days?
To calm the nerves, we so needed
one yoga class a week, just
an hour alone before we picked up
a whirl of toys, drew baths,
read stories, paid bills, scrubbed dishes
and spoke for two minutes on the phone
with a friend.  Later, time for one glass
of wine, the garbage out for tomorrow,
and a single thought for a poem
hovering.  *God*, I prayed, let me sleep
well tonight before I start again.

# Stones

The things we do in graveyards—
these days, I touch smooth granite
and finger letters, birth dates carved in stone.
I only touch; tears gone.

At seventeen we drove
to the cemetery and made love our first time
as the radio intoned that Bobby Kennedy
was dead.  A hundred sudden ghosts
rose up and wailed around us.

Childhood was my highlight
among the dead.  I biked and hopped from
stone to stone, then sat in shade and ate
raspberries picked along the way.

*Look*, I said to the surrounding space,
*I'm watching over all of you!*
Only the wind spoke as I biked home,
a seven-year-old who thought of graveyards
as a poem.

# My Once and Future Lovers

I loved you all.

That first kiss at thirteen, my lips
shaky-nervous, tiny hairs
on my cheek raised by thrill,
by bliss.

At nineteen I married you
my lord, you.  Like the River Merchant's Wife,
my bangs cut straight across my forehead,
dark braids falling down my back.
Oh, the days, the nights, you made stars pulse for me!

When I cheated at thirty, ugliness
reared its dark shoulders.  When you cheated
not long after, flames erupted everywhere.

At forty-three, my boy was your boy's
age.  We sledded, bowled and biked
with them, then spent nights
in the deep heat of bed while they slept.

Again at fifty-five I found you, a man
who texted poems to me.  You nursed me
through a knee replacement, the world of love
a little different at this age.

And if I ever stumble upon you again
I'd ask for something simple—
companionship, say, two people
cooking dinner together

or tending to the yard, affection
the low steady current running between us

like an underground fire.

# Light Rolling Slowly Backward

It's August, the season of regret,
the season of late beauty brittling
on the edge, months before
the frost.  Crickets drone
their low nighttime hum

and sadness passes like a light
wind through the windows.
What is it that we miss?
The lilies are long gone,
but phlox blooms deep pink
and cosmos sway
their bright yellow hearts out.

It's August and we're hurtling
toward November, even as
the glory burst of Fall color lies ahead.
Light rolls slowly backward now
while days shorten.  Our shadows grow.

In high school, I remember memorizing
*Margaret, are you grieving*
*over Goldengrove unleaving?*

That must be what this mourning is,
days away from what's to come,
even as the crickets chirr
their bright summer song.

*Love, if I knew you, ever found you—*

# Claddagh

The Claddagh ring is a traditional Irish ring. The hands represent friendship, the heart represents love, and the crown represents loyalty. The design and customs associated with it originated in the Irish fishing village of the same name in Galway. The ring, as currently known, was first produced in the 17th century.

And I imagined the moon
as a Claddagh ring,
dipped in gold with a heart
at the bottom and a crown
on top, two hands wound
around it. It reeled me back
to Ireland, when in childhood
I learned the place-name *Claddagh*,
the tiny fishing village
where the river Corrib meets
Galway Bay. I can still see
its brick rowhouses today.

Tonight the moon is fierce
and I am missing you
again, your two arms
wound around me all night
long. So many years
back, you turned to me
and said that every midnight
you wished the clock
would stop and we could lie
together always.

Today I wear the Claddagh ring
on my right hand, while your wife
wears it on her left. All night the gulls
make sorrowful noises above
the Bay. You live in the west
of Ireland now, while I have chosen
the broad American prairies
far from the sea.

# Guest

Step inside your longing and see
        how spacious is the room,

how light slants spillingly
        on every surface,

how liquid the longing is.
        Once in a lifetime—twice,

maybe, if we're lucky—
        we enter the quiet zero

of love's center.  All the dazzle and grind,
        bustle, lure and fray of outward things

peels away, falls to the wayside
        like dry November leaves.

The blue orb of the heart's silence
        waits, a house alone.

It brushes our shoulders
        with a blanket of stars

and we are stunned into speechlessness
        at such privilege. This is the dwelling

we have longed for all our lives.
        *Let me be your guest, love*

we whisper in our gratitude.
        *Only let me be your guest.*

# Middle Age Looks Back

*Zipolite, Oaxaca*

We walk the beach for hours,
slipping now and then into the sea
to rinse away the sand.

We are young, we are bright,
we are brash and crazy-happy,
our lasso-love like golden hoops

around us, breaking all we touch
into light.  We will never be
this age again, will never know

such strong magic. Beat and roll
you thunderous Pacific waves, you
riptide pull beneath our feet,

you'll never catch us.

# Our 8th Grade Girl Scout Trip to Chicago

We weren't hookers.
We were thirteen-year-old girl scouts out on a dare
in our brand-new flats, trench coats over nighties,
buying Cokes for our friends.

The Chicago police
thought otherwise and were a little rude,
shoving us into a back seat
locked and speeding toward our troop leader
at the Pearl Hotel.

My nylons were ruined
and my heart lurched furiously.
Sara and I feared the punishment
our parents might mete out
upon our return to St. Paul. Our troop
leader said she'd tell the whole
of St. Luke's School, she'd *had* it
with us.

Not sure what happened to Sara
when we got back. Me, I was grounded
for a year from Bober's Drugstore
with its sweet fountain
cherry phosphates.  And I never
told my kids this story,
and I probably never will.

# The Heart-Whisperer

*for Susan, again*

Four years ago he died, my youngest
half-hidden pride, a boy of twenty-three.
Four years ago, you took me in, no notice,
a surprise at your New England door,
and you gently scrubbed the hurt from me
all week as I grieved.  Friend, I think I knew you
before birth, some rare bond we found
again that summer we met at Frost Place.
I think of you today, your rich, uncanny poems
always with me, your generosity
a tent you spun above me giving shelter.
And I think of my boy, gone now,
and how I wish, Susan, that he'd met you.

# All the Ways of Sorry

For all the men I loved
but never slept with, I'm sorry.
For the way the sun rose, pale
and empty the day my son died,
I'm sorry.  For what has happened
in the Arctic that's beyond my reach
to alter, I am sorry.  For
the creeping Charlie which I lost
the battle to, I'm also sorry.
For the president who hurt my country
into broken bits, I am deeply
sorry.  For the time I didn't take
that day when you were just
in kindergarten—I'm sorry.
For all the zings and hurts
in our friendship when we were
just fourteen, I'm sorry.  For the children
at the border parentless in cages,
I am more than sorry.  For George Floyd's
dead body, oh my God, I'm sorry.
For the sky just as it was then, blue
and buoyant at the first loss years back,
I am so sorry.

# Melancholia, Round 23

Last night I saw an animal
just outside my bedroom window
and for an instant I felt doomed.
*Go away, black squirrel.*

Today the tiny hooks
bite, little jabs     beneath
the surface; the squeezed-grey
Sundays, ruined boots        submerged
beneath black water.

How many times can we try,
try, for the bright spirit
that fails     once again     when we can't
see the sun the way the rest can?
I can't count the ways I can't.

Numbness blurs. For a minute
beneath the quilt, I am happy
before I remember I am not—
and every spark forward retreats
to blankness.

*But oh, the mind,*
*mind has mountains, cliffs of fall,*
Hopkins said.

I get up reeling,
knowing the way up is     long
and my feet are raw infants
at the mountain base.

# Lewy Bodies

At the intersection
of dementia and clarity,
in the wood where light is faltering,
near the cliff that separates
the upright from the fallen, wolves
are calling for my father's passage.

I hear his name bandied with the others
and I wince.  We joke about
the "minder" who's been hired,
Bob, his large hands, maternal soul.
*At least he reads*, my father says,
*though work's impossible when he is here.*

For now there is a safety zone
of small dimension like a plank
where my father balances, staggers
a little dazed at moments, the vigor
of his past behind him, the long slide ahead.

# Summer Ants

Those miniscule brown soldiers,
my kitchen ants. Around
and around they go, swarming
on drops of Terro ant killer,
drunk on clear, sweet goo.

If I had a needle, I'd say
they were thread, infinitesimally
slight, waving their long skein
back and forth in lilliputian motion.
Here is one, slim as an eyelash,
moving toward the bait.

By morning they'll be delirious
on the stuff. Come night,
most will disappear back to their homes
and die. The rest will follow

and the cats will be emancipated
from the basement where they were
quarantined for their own protection
against the sweet goo

they'd probably want to dive into
and lick before the usual licking
of each other. Ah, those ants.

And cats.

# The Summer I Wanted to Be a Boy

I cut my hair shorter than a pixie's
and wore boys' clothes the year
I turned eleven.   I knew where the power lay
even as a child, and I wanted it.  Boys
could fart and get their shorts muddy,
bang other boys' ears, stay out after dark.
I envied them and their loose boy ways.

I ditched skirts and wore my brother's
baseball cap.  I hid my panties
inside boxers.   That July
my aunt coaxed me into a dress
which flew sky-high on the Staten Island
ferry, and my multi-covered bottom mooned
the laughing passengers.

It didn't last.  Adolescence
brought the same surge of hormones
any boy had, and I gave it up
to my teenaged beau.  I was sure
he loved me as much as I loved him.

Flash forward to adulthood
where men in ties around the table
ruled without question, where
the only currency spent was by and for
those men, where women squirmed beneath
the stained paws of Brett Kavanaghs,

where we carried the memory
of being shut out from the treehouse,
barred from baseball fields
and boardrooms, made to feel invisible
even in our own marriages –

What did I possibly know
when I was just eleven?

# I Can't Breathe

*for George Floyd*

All week the helicopters whir and drone
until they feel like wasps
inside my head, until they lodge in hot bits
inside my ribs, until they take me back to Vietnam
when Jeff was dying high above the gauzy clouds
in that Huey chopper.

Sirens scream down the streets
and we smell the smoke that curls
from torched buildings.  Look at us,
America in 2020, no different from
the year we lynched Emmett Till in 1955.

Today I mourn the death
of George Floyd, whose neck
was pinned for nine minutes
beneath a white cop's knee
until the only thing that could be heard
was "I can't breathe." I mourn
the officers who didn't try to help
him, I mourn everyone
who didn't get the news in time
to intervene or yell "stop!"

For the residue of the lynching tree
in the blood of those who killed him,
for the brutal fires and looting that came next;
for my dear neighborhood in ruins
and for the small businesses
that just couldn't bear the weight;
for the fury of provocateurs
who torched peaceful protests
with their hate, I toss my own
grenade of grief up to the sky.

# The Radiation Room

Here in November
during this dark Advent,
gathered on the ceiling overhead
I can see
the stars of summer:
Aquila, Lyra and Hercules.
Little pings of light, with
beams that sweep my chest
(yes, lovingly)
while a red light slices side to side
looking for its mark.

Eyes closed now,
the constellations are
everyone I've ever loved—
family, friends, poets dead and alive,
the child next door, my homeless clients
on the Greenway in their tents, even the freckled guy
at the grocery store with the kind smile.

They are my relatives, my light
my golden wheat swaying in the wind,
moving toward me,
saying *it's all right.*

In a month the winter constellations
will come to show their faces—Canis Major,
Gemini, Orion and the others.
And after my turn, surely there'll be
a new tenant on this table
to study the steady lights
of stars above, whispering
their reassuring names.

*from*
# Caravan

(Midwest Villages and Voices
*and* Dedalus Press, 1989)

# Still-Life on Inisheer

*from "The Island Poems"*

In the low stone houses,
the dream-fires begin to stir.
Somewhere from sleep, an old woman sighs
and laughs for sheer release,
circling back beneath the ice
to greener years.

She does not hear her husband rise
and wind his woollen way
down toward the blue-throated sea,
where his bony curraghs
huddle on the sand
like a pair of hands curved in prayer.

He is a nightwalker:
says he feels some days a strange decay
has settled in upon the island
like an old neighbor coming home to die.
He will fish now in darkness, riding out
where the waters clear themselves of ghosts.

She has made her peace with sleep,
and turns above her pillows
to embrace familiar ghosts,
dreaming the island and she are aged whispers
whittled from an older roar,
with all their edges honed and muted down
till they've become like sand or air.

An ancient moon trembles
and silhouettes the woollen man
in chalky tones.
He lays his wrinkled cheek upon his mounded nets,
and lets himself drift
further and further from home.

# Céilí Mór

*from "The Island Poems"*

Half daft with music,
flushed with drink,
sweaty as cows at yesterday's market

we spun all night in giddy step
and stamped our neighbors' toes
three inches to the left.

The band played reels and waltzes
till the breathless crowd had stopped;
the arms around waists were prizes carried off.

Then hours afterward, just this—
two bodies in an empty room
still circling in around desire

toward the prize not given yet,
that final dance
into the liquid elegance of sex.

# To Inishmore

*from "The Island Poems"*

The boat engines whir and hum
and the gangplank scrapes shut.
Someone is always leaving, leaving—

In Mexico, the child cries to its mother
as the train pulls away, while somewhere else,
perhaps, events and bodies gladly break apart.

Above the ship, gulls are thrashing the air
to bits.  Their high calls
slice the air like knives, a Greek chorus.

Did the woman in the black dress there
leaning toward the wind,
fall, last night,

before she closed her eyes,
to that old lie
of softness in dark?

Remote, awkward today,
empty of promises
as the grey Galway sky,

we'll part strangers again,
blank as the creamy surf
that rings the ship sides

as your boat glides out into the distance.

# All Together Now

OK friends, I'll ask my selves
just how it was we came to this:

Before, believe me, I sang
beneath the willows in the kind emperor's court
in China, the year before I fell from grace
for making silver sounds that unbound women's feet;
a mystery to me.  For this I was exiled,
and though centuries have kited by, I still see
the emperor awake in the canopied bed, each fluid note
I taught him fretting through his head.

Or the years in France, the grapes
purpling my skin
right through to cells in fingertips,
clutch, snip and a clump in the bucket;
kneeling in mud through rain-crazed days,
of raw-handed weariness till
the sweet crop began its other life
away from earth, pointed wineward
toward American fluorescence, *grand cru* style.

Remember Veracruz!  I played marimba
in the Zocalo, and every night whirled by
in Panacolor, only the Gringos grey
in pale discussion over black coral
necklaces: how many pesos, Señor?
We plunked the keys and beat the drums
till dawn rose like a new oil field,
gold flames that lit the waves
breaking on the Gulf.

Then here, to the city of wind-chill factors,
where I finally gave it up to the boys of the prairie;
thought seriously about loons and compost heaps,
unlearned dance and poetry; shed my old street life.
Now I flatten daily, thinner than peeled garlic skin,

barely squeaking in
through the stern Scandinavian door.
My personas grow confused (what land is this?)
homesick for song, black dirt, and Mexican waterfront.
I tell you friend, this time I'm determined
to conform: punch the clock and hear alarms,
visit the animals on the farm.  And if the last
schizophrenic one of me refuses to be tamed, the one
who yearns to hitch-hike back to the Pacific,
then I say let's throw her on a raft
to the wild muskies in Lake Harriet.
When we meet again, integration
and stability just might set in,

and those other transients I own
can hop the next train south.
Then all the sisters, brothers of my separate selves
who bear the marks of older scattered lives
in foreign parts will bow before the mayor
and be granted permanent asylum.
We'll take the oath with one lid closed,
we're here to stay, as one,
or two...or three...no promises given; just maybe.

# Winter Widower in Key West

What remains now
in memory
under constant mild sun
is the sheer abandon of it then:

not the bitter days of snow
stiff-casketed
against New England windowsills;
nor the calves' writhings

finally stilled to ghosted forms
like rigid plants
statued white by wind
lassoing drifts under their feet;

not even that blackest winter
that the years won't erase,
when pneumonia seized the child
by degrees, like dropping mercury—

bright petal, paler petal,
brittle curlings on the ground.
Then, Mary, you broke too, just wilted
like the frost-hurt yellow roses

we grieved piece by falling piece
in the aging summer of our last heat,
when afterward, you joined them
underground.

Here, an old man deserves reprieve:
the mindless lap of waves,
noon naps in winter sun,
an afternoon martini in the shade.
But that abandon: oh, when we were young,
we threw ourselves three feet deep
into the snow, making angel arcs
*en route* to China we believed below.

And we hunted snowflakes by the net,
giddy with hysteria, release,
strong bones triumphant
with that landbound catch,

some heady spininess
to us then, some raw angularity
alien to winter
in Key West.

# St. James Orphan

*"It was surrounded by enormous high prison-like walls. Entrance was gained through a great doorway, permanently closed. It was in this doorway, a century or so ago, that a little revolving contraption had been inserted into which mothers placed babies for whom they could no longer care. By turning it around, they could send the little child into the awful prospect of almost certain death in the workhouse."*

from *Against the Tide*, Noel

Browne

MOTHER

As if we had a choice.
The three-penny upright on the street
who lifts her tired skirts to faceless men
a dozen times a day doesn't choose either; no more
than my body planned to spill out
five weak babies, the lump sum
of my husband's blunt hunger.

I've seen their faces
in the shadows of St. James,
those other mothers parting with young flesh.
If looks could kill, this city'd reek
of death.

You were my smallest one,
little runt among the sparrows,
lame last-born girl.
"Suffer the children," Father Conroy says,
but I don't believe it any more.

CHILD

They wake you arguing.
You've heard the words so many times
by now they seem a lullabye:
too many mouths, the bread's run out,
no coal, one boy, three girls,
another girl.
The song ends like a warped psalm.
And you sleep.

Your mama whispers that it's just a dream,
dresses you in winter knickers,
the Sunday-best grey dress. Her kisses
heat the pre-dawn cold. You sleepwalk
through the Dublin slums
to walls that block the sky of light,

then she lets go your hand.
One world ends
as you watch your mother's face
closing for the last time
while the small shelf
slowly swings you into darkness.

# For Naoise Unborn

First one, little fish,
you kick and dart and glide
beneath my ribs
as if they were your private reef.

For months I've felt you fatten
like a mollusk,
each swell and bump of you
a new pearl.

Sea-newt, limpet-child
I've never known,
I am your mother ocean:
my arms are waves

holding you, I rock
your tiny bones
inside the brine.
Sleep here, you're home.

# Going Back

Here: it must be where you stood,
one hand raised to shade your eyes
against the harsh Atlantic
grinding shoulders with the rocks below.

How your skirt cut the wind in half!
And how you waited, brooding
for the boats that stitched their slow way in
with ribboned wakes a deeper green,
and each new ship
a promise that you couldn't keep.

I see the girl you were walk back alone
to her father's house,
caught between two hungers.
Some absent strain of music kept you restless,
and I know how the longing worked on you,
for even at night
the boats sent out a siren tongue—
foreign to your ear, perhaps, but song.

One day you finally left,
sailing your boat straight into the cave
of America's open arms;
feeling the wind no monster
there, after such lean dreams
as you had culled from Irish soil.

Mama Mór, I stand here now
where you once stood,
the unchanged land beneath my feet,
certain that my bones were formed
from that same air
that made your bones first stir.
But the old heritage breeds a different pain in me:
a stranger to both countries,
I cannot make my roots take hold;
can only stand and hear the sea
return the poems that you'd willed it
as a child, while the wind
raises ghosts behind me.

# Arctic Expedition

Instead of hands, we held
ropes in human chain
fastened ten feet down the line
to each man's wrist.

When the white-outs came, snow
closed our throats and severed vision
back to camp.  Then, we'd wrestle terror
worse than any avalanche.

It's six long months
since the bush pilot dropped us
cleanly to our gear, and the folly
we'd imagined an explorer's glory.

Today his battered Cessna's scheduled to return.
Once home, I'll steel-wool the fungi
off my unwashed chest
and never dream again, please God,

of the moment when the rope slackened
and the first of us was lost to wolves,
some said; though I alone carry the load
of a snow-stunned act: the letting go his cord.

# My Mother's Hands

I lift the nightgown over my head
but it is my mother's hands I hear instead.
Thirty years back, her fingers are quiet burrs
snagging small rips through the silences
of folded laundry piles, a sandpapery bristle
against old lingerie, softened linens,
even the stiff diapers of the ninth child.

I swore then *my* hands would escape
cream-smooth into adulthood,
not knowing, Mother, how the body
disobeys in time; how skin roughens,
tears and cracks past boundaries of repair,
how at a certain stage this woman's hands
would rasp the same tune on flannel
as your own.

# History of Proper Nouns

*at the Vietnam War Memorial, Washington, D.C., 1987*

They are so small from here—
*John Anderson   Earl Bernhardt   James E Bates*
ankle-high letters on a black marble wall,
the plain annunciation of names
of the first three American dead.

It must have begun as simply as this,
one inch, one foot at a time,
till boots lost track of distance
and fell feet up into months, into years,
into the last blank stare of space.

The wall steepens on the path down
as spotlights brightens thousands more names.
Their letters breed above my head
like a disease: *Michael   Phillip   Robert   Séan*
a litany of lives dwarfed to characters on stone.

And for an instant, Hades overwhelms
the mild sunlight of a winter's day, surreal
and terrible, as if a dark grenade of language
holding each casket stretched underground
from Maine to Arkansas,

from Oregon to Florida,
had exploded and rained down some mute lexicon
of syllables long since grown cold; as if
Jim Morrison had walked back from dead, singing
*This is the end, my beautiful friend . . . .*

A second layer of black marble and the wall stops.
Stepping into daylight, the brisk sky is so blue
it almost bites, and the burnt-gold flowers
lying at the last name glow
like the aftershock of light at dusk

or the heated glitter in a young man's eyes
open and blind at noon in a jungle forest.

# Instruction from a Self-Made Mentor

The poet told me if I were serious,
I would isolate myself
and would eat nothing but almonds
soaked in white wine
for a year and three days.
He said this recipe had certainty,
would bleach the mind
and sharpen it for revelation.

Anyone could sense his gravity;
he offered wisdom
as though it were some precious essence
to hoard through a shortage.
His hair was white
and his eyes were bright,
though somewhat hard.
I knew he'd learned the secrets long ago.

So I readied myself for a vision quest,
solemn and wide-eyed and ripe.
I set up a shrine to Orpheus
and did my incantation daily.
I ate almonds till my tongue was white
and clean and smooth,
like the heart of one, split open.
Then I turned to wine
and purified myself some more.

The poet built his life on this.
Now he drives an El Dorado
and rubs his pockets fondly,
dreaming of the next edition
of messages and myths
for serious young poets.
Last time I saw him, he winked.
I did what I had to do:
I shot him with my .22.

# House/Light

Meagre, but delirious with light—
a house lit by gladiolas in a perfect urn,
blossoms floating in a saucer in the bedroom.

Dreaming, I've entered this house before
a dozen times, testing each spring and gleam
of oak floor for permanence; the high-set windows

for possibilities of truth they may disclose,
the slant of light for certain angles
that might nurture indoor garden growth.

Yet something in the broad prairie
that these rooms suggest
must be a trick of structure only

and I still resist believing that I hear
the walls whispering *come in, come in,*
*mo chroí,* you're home, you're free.

Visiting, I've heard the low flutter
of a restless bird in the attic, troubled
by her struggle whether she should leave or stay.

Dreams claim these houses are pieces
of our used psyches, buildings we erect
from planks or shingles pried loose

from the sleeping mind's cave,
until they grow themselves
into dwellings we already knew

but couldn't yet recognize awake.
I don't know—some nights
I think I'm growing closer

as I practice small steps forward
toward the leap I want to make—
from primate speech of dreams

into the language that I'd rather speak,
walking syllable by bright syllable
into the house which utters light,

to the man carrying blazing flowers,
house, house, light, light,
the heavy dove of harmony

resting gently on my shoulders,
claws asleep,
at peace.

# Dancing the Boys into Bed

Crazy with giggles, a knee-high tornado
is dancing my skirt into knots.
His younger brother's slung across my shoulder,
bobbing his head to some infant dream.

They are the princes of Baba
and I am the palace queen
with regal peanut butter on her cheek.
We are kissing the world goodnight,

skimming a child's cha-cha
across he wooden floor, prancing our feet
to the beat of the baby's hiccups
in the bedtime world of Baba.

Sway, boys, rock the giddy room
to bits. I'll blanket down the castle
and toss some stars above your cribs,
then gently dance you into sleep.

*from*

# The One Who Swears
# You Can't Start Over

(Salmon Poetry, 2002)

# Barn Burning

The barn burned all night,
its black ribs alive and bare
against the orange glow.
How I wanted to enter
its great light, to slip on
the exquisite dress sewn
from tips of flame, test
the weightless shoes of white ash
waiting there for me
since birth.
When the hulk of roof
finally fell in hot chunks
at my feet, I would pocket
two small pieces of its history
and walk unscathed
out to the long wet grasses
just beyond the barn,
where I would press my body
to the green earth
until it seared an imprint
there.  And then I would
memorize
again and yet again
the outline of the lit barn
and its lean bones;
the world charged suddenly
as baptism, my life changed
forever with the knowledge
of fire.

# The Otherworld

Only ninety steps from house to forest.
I counted them, summer days, my whole body
pulled like a magnet toward the green light
humming through the thick stand of pines.
It was the otherworld I craved, the air
silver with dust motes floating down between
deep green needles, the pitch of pine scent
tuned tightly to a high thin note,
the forest floor worn and soft as an old rug,
and all the lure of foreign places calling.

We danced there, my sisters and I,
twirling our gypsy skirts for an audience
of mute trees in the clearing.  By noon
we were heady with possibility
of claiming the lost Irish crown, the coveted role
of Queen Kathleen, Ruler of the Forest.

And each day ended with my mother's voice
sounding the dinner call, pulling us back
again.  While we ate, while
we played, every hour surged forward
and away from us into the future,
and never once as we filled our lungs
with great gulps of sweet green air
did we consider this.

# Dress-Ups

I was the gypsy with the mismatched scarves,
torn petticoats and practiced foreign air.
Nuala was the princess, her blue-black hair
like night on snow, regal curls tumbling down
around the cape my mother had fashioned
from the white lace slip she hadn't worn
since the ninth child's birth.

A coven of giggly girls we were, deep
in the land of dress-ups, pure babes
at the altar of artifice, the sweet
imaginary world of grown-up women
sensed through fingertips as we stroked pink
organza, cinched the faded blue satin blouse
around our waists with old rope, dreamed
of marriages we wouldn't yet know for years,
of silky nights of August heat
with our discarded costumes flung
across some chair, skins bare at last
of any fabric but the soft chenille coverlet
resting on our legs.

# Those Girls

They never learn, those girls.
At seven, shut out from the clubhouse,
they simply wait it out.
Come fourteen, each one
will allow some boy
the buttons to her blouse, believing
certainly, he loves her now.
They fall hard, marry early
and at thirty wonder
where the years went,
why their longing lingers still.

Women now, they spend their thirst
on men who cannot quench it,
cowboys with deserts in their hearts.
The sun sets and rises; sets again
to men who daily break these women open
with unfaithfulness, a nod, a fist,
a word, the silence of refusal
or a simple walk away.

Those girls, they'll never learn,
their eyes mesmerized and glittering
with moon.  I watch their moth-like arms
reaching outward to the fire, watch
them singe and burn with pain
every time they stretch those arms
toward that reckless red flame
some call love.

# Beginning To Name It: Poetry

It is the strange vegetable
that grows outside the garden,
at once pocked and luminous.
It is the one nutrient
your body longs for
when you feel nothing
but hunger and desire,
bent double with the need
for even a morsel of its blue leaves.
It is the mystery scientists
spend late-night hours researching
and the speech of wind in an empty room;
it falls from the sleeping child's mouth
in a whimper or a sigh, it lies
quietly in file cabinets, the small ink
alphabets pulsing straight through metal.
And at any moment in this world
it can seize you with its reckless song
or water the desert hidden
in your heart.  Shyly, it may ask you
for the next dance alone
and at evening's end, brand you
with the fire of its necessary name.

# Why I Lied My Way Through Childhood

Because I loved the textured detail
fiction added to the ordinary real,
the dull navy Easter coat embroidered
with elaborate gold brocade instead.
Because I'd read *Pippi Longstocking*
so many times I couldn't help believe
she truly was my cousin and we'd lived
together every summer on that island.
Because the landscape of fact was plain
as fishstick-Fridays in Lent, and what harm
was there imagining I'd turned the dial
on Mrs. Hewitt's birth-control pills
a few notches forward when babysitting,
bragging to disbelieving friends
there'd be another baby in the year?
Because I *liked* the sympathy the nuns
doled like warm honey when they learned
I had leukemia at sixteen.
Because it's well-known the Irish are prone
to hyperbole, and because my parents
refused me acting lessons, holding out
for violin.  Because I always wanted
the world to be bigger than it is.
Telling my children tonight about the time
I won Merlin's sword in a stone-toss,
I know they know this is the utter truth
from Mom's childhood.

# The Poet Finds New Formulae

*—after a remark by Robert Bly about his new working*
*ritual of writing a poem a day in bed before arising,*
*enjoying his coffee as he writes—*

In my retirement, I, too, vow to write
a poem a day before leaving bed.
There will be coffee first, of course, heaped
with cream and served by a young man
eager to please.  Three gulps I need before
the words can even start homing in
toward the poem... Then I'll stretch and drink
and consider the placement of commas,
debate with myself about whether the epic
or the lyric is best-suited for the day.
When the poem's done and all the coffee
gone, the young man will draw my bath
and I will arise bursting with virtue,
humming with caffeine, grateful
for the training my young man received
before landing his internship
with this older poet sailing in her prime.

How tiresome it gets amidst these covers
in the afternoon sun!  Long past noon
and I'm still drumming an arthritic finger
on blank paper, pleading with recalcitrant
words which will not line up with the others,
pounding stubborn images into bloom.  Fury
builds in me as I cancel one appointment,
then the next.  When the boys asks discreetly
whether Madam wishes for an afternoon snack,
something snaps and I yank his hair,
then call the agency, demanding
a replacement.  Oh, to write one sestina
by the time night falls—to toss the stale coffee
down the drain, peel back the years and start again!

# Snow White Revived

"Mirror, mirror on the wall"
was how the whole thing started,
my stepmother trembling at the threshold
of middle age, her radiant beauty
just about to fade.  Innocent
of the mirror's lure, I wore my black hair
in straight braids, knew each tree
in the forest by its bark, conversed
with thrush and lark as I played.

So you can see that when the prince
plucked the poisonous apple
from between my lips,
I couldn't bear the joy in his eyes.
What lay ahead was someone else's destiny,
tiresome curtseys and the weight of a crown;
a closet full of wasp-waisted dresses
and villagers "your highnessing" me
right and left, with all the expectations
of a man who'd saved my life
waiting for me in bed at night.

All I'd really wanted was to dwell
in harmony among the dwarves,
playing Scrabble at the breakfast table
with the little men I loved, Doc and Sleepy
waving as they walked out the door
to the mines, Bashful and Dopey
singing a duet while we washed the morning dishes.

But the drama's fizzled into history
long ago—the huntsman who spared my neck,
the trick of combs and apples, the fact
of my survival. God knows why,
but one morning I unbound my braids
and stepped into the palace for the first time.

My hair slid down my shoulders
and I shivered as it settled
on the weight of red brocade below.

How I miss playing house
with that band of doting dwarves,
how I can't explain to Hans
I preferred the apple in my throat
to this queenship I pretend is mine.

# Peter Flees Galilee for the Mountains

Can I tell you what the journey has been like?
My sandals nearly ground to dust,
my legs heavy as stone pillars
at day's end, the robust sea air
leaving my lungs which fill instead
with the thin broth of high altitude.

Everything was simple before
he said my name: *Peter*, like that,
and suddenly my life of nets
and fish diminished into gestures
of no consequence.
The broad sea lost its lustre,
the sun flattened out the hills
and I was his.

Now I have been travelling for weeks
to escape his face, that voice
an arrow shooting toward my boat,
my shuttered heart, homing in
on every hidden cell.

I thought that once out of my element
I'd forget, the bulk and height of land
above my head so foreign
it would obliterate the past
with its sheer mass, its power.

But when I press my skin
against the granite cheeks of the mountain
I hear him deep inside the rock,
calling me again.
Lord, is there nowhere on this earth
that I can hide?

# Alzheimer's Weather

*"I think sometimes it's as if a storm were going through*
*her head and she doesn't even know it."*

—my father, on the telephone last night—

At first the weather was mild,
scattered showers at most
or the occasional dim hint of lightning.
She'd laugh when she'd forgotten
where she parked the car,
and so would we.

Lately now it seems a kind of static's
playing havoc with her brain
as small gaps of time explode into oblivion,
the way the weight of January snow
snapped the one brittle branch
off the burr oak last year
and suddenly a space blank as loss appeared
among the tangle of black branches.

All my life I've been afraid of thunder,
hiding, once, under my desk at 2:00 a.m.
in the old place on Selby over Captain Ken's.
I don't know why she doesn't reel or jump
the way I do when it booms through the sky,
or whether it's just one more sound
added to the clamor humming there
between her ears.

How I'd like to hold her as the slow tornado
approaches, how we'd all like to save her
from the darkness of the storm.
But her children have become remote
as third cousins, blurred shadows
indistinct as any raindrops
splashed on summer windows.

The burden of memory is to feel pain:
I pray she doesn't own it.  Let her mistake
me for her sister and I'll gladly answer
in the present tense; let my father's banter
serve as courtship once again.  Let
her small world keep her safe from any harm,
and in the stillness of amnesia
let her never know the sting or fury
of the desert wind.

# Theft

Last night I stole her blue beaded necklace,
the one I'd given her some past Christmas.
While she sat in her favorite flowered chair
tracking dust motes under the table lamp,
I slipped the string of beads
into the zipper pocket of my black purse.

When the dead leave, what is left to clutch?
All the rough intangibles become so much dust,
flour sifting downward from a torn bag.
Some raw material thing becomes necessity,
an article which owns the memory of perfume
or holds the far remembered cry of a voice
calling us in summer on the fevered afternoons
we'd stray too deep into the lake.

She won't miss it now, the necklace,
a minor theft when held against this largest loss
of all.  I watch her press her hands to her head
asking where in God's name it has disappeared,
who has sacked her life and carried off her very mind,
who the robber, what the theft, when the larceny occurred,
Jesus, why.

# Birthday

At 75, she's a small girl again,
singing her own "happy birthday"
as we lay the cake before her.
Candles light her eyes the way
they did at ten, when the pretty curls
her mother brushed spun loops around her head.

It's so confusing who the birthday girl
is, so many children mixing up
the present with the past.  My thin father
tells her that he loves her,
and she becomes nineteen
in pale blue formal dress, anxious
as she brushes flecks of dirt from white gloves
in the subways of New York
where they will meet in 1935.

Now she walks across the dining room
to a photo of an older sister,
kisses it and turns to us as if
the keeper of a grand secret.
"I like this girl," she says, "because
her family's so polite, because she always
buys me nice clothes."

When everyone has left and hours have passed
since my sisters sanely entered sleep,
she'll pull her bureau scarf and all
her pretty jars roughly to the floor
and she will scream.  I've become the demon

that I always was to her,
she'll threaten the police unless
I bring my father back again,
she'll rant and weep and plead for different
years,

she'll smash the green Belgian glass
two inches from my head
even as she curses this disease,

a pained, heavy woman
in her 76th year, holding me,
the difficult daughter incapable of tears.

# Absences

Cell by cell my mother is leaving us.
No one can stop the memory leaking
from her body in such helpless cupfuls,
the way flecks of dead skin disappear
and scatter into air like loose dust gone wild
when brushed from sun-dried flesh.

The lost language in her eyes,
my face before hers like a question-mark,
her vision blank with Haldol
or bright with terror,
a terrible incomprehension
stuttering through her body—

I hear the doctors say her brain
has atrophied a few degrees
beyond the CT scan of last year,
and I see a border of grey air
circling that unprotected, shrunken mass,
empty spaces wind could rattle through,
small animals could chatter in.

The howl at the door. Each day, every night.
Down the road, a gravesite beckoning.
My body like a fetus, curled in mute rage
on the floor near her bed. Selfish
as an infant, wondering who will know us now,
when we were children.

My mother, in all her Irish beauty,
singing suddenly at 3:00 a.m.:
*"The violets were scenting the woods, Maggie,*
*displaying their charms to the breeze,*
*when I first said I loved only you, Maggie,*
*and you said you loved only me."*
My father, weeping.

# Night Shift

She went down like an angel into sleep
tonight, serene and rosy after dinner,
every struggle of the day a deep
thing shrugged away into the blur
of slumber.  Such gifts as this are pure
jewels after nights of strain,
weeks of fending off dementia's gain.

# Potatoes

Someone is weeping in the kitchen.
It is my father, crying quietly
as he peels the dinner potatoes.
He pierces their white hearts with a fork
and steam rises upward toward his beard.
Below, hot tears salt the bowl.
The intimacy of the moment staggers,
as when I stumbled, once, as a child,
upon him cupping my mother's face
in broad, noon daylight as they entered
the deep, private zone of a kiss.
How could he have known, when he made
that vow fifty seven years ago,
how suddenly and readily she'd leave him—
pork chops burnt, potatoes blackening
over gas—for that thin stranger
called Alzheimer, waltzing through
the kitchen door like a suitor
who has never lost a single lover's hand
he's played?

# The Other Woman, Revisited

So now he's back again and you become
the same fool you were once before
but doubly so, with all the benefits
of insight that a decade should accrue.
Funny how the landscape hasn't altered,
the woods of self-deceit still green
and winsome with their pretty paths leading
nowhere, and all the trees bent with promises,
their disappointing fruit unripened yet.
But it's sweeter in the forest
on that bed of leaves where he makes love
to you on lunch hours, easier
somehow to stay than to leave
for that other world where you must trail
him ten feet back in a crowd, worrying
about the fresh smudge of earth on his suitcoat
that his wife or someone in the office
might detect, and trying to balance that
against the child thickening in your belly
whose faint, bewildered cries will one day grow
to howls for the father whom he'll never know.

# Through the Looking Glass

*Castlehaven Cabins, Lake Superior*

The window over the lake was streaked with rain,
a violent sideways slash of wetness
gusting upward.  But I could see Superior
well enough to want to lose myself
in its great embrace; could see you, too,
writing steadily in your left-handed stance
at the cabin table.
White caps raised the waves beyond the shore
to beaten peaks and the Great Lake
frothed and turned, a huge, relentless motion
echoing back upon itself.

Something happened as I sat.  I can't say what,
exactly, but some willing crack inside my mind
opened to the grey force outside me
and I slipped right through it
to the world between two worlds, that country
just beyond the looking-glass.
It was the future that I saw, love,
and you weren't in it, anywhere.
The boys and I were older, walking down a summer road
alone, and we wore that raw look of peace
survivors wear as they leave the burning house
without scars.  We held hands tightly,
heading home.

I watched us travelling without you
and felt such sadness for what might have been
that I nearly turned and told you what I'd seen.
I watched myself watching all of this
and knew with helpless certainty
I couldn't stop what hadn't yet occurred.
I watched the rain bead to bubble on the glass
and burst, watched Superior blacken
into sudden night and finally felt
my legs asleep beneath me in the big chair.
Your notebook was black and fat with words
and your back was turned from me,
completely unaware of where I'd been.

# The Window of Regret

We would always wish it to be otherwise.
That the four food groups lived in pleasant harmony
in our daily lives and our bodies pure
from working out; that we'd bagged the trash
the night before and hauled it down
before the garbage trucks arrived at dawn.
That we'd heeded hurricane warnings,
dropped the whole material past and left
with souls intact.  Or spoken crucial words
to a friend before the plane roared away
and it was suddenly too late.  That our parents
knew the full dimension of our love
while they were still most alive.
That one or both of us had shown more faith
and the twin stems our bodies were
had not conceived such rancor or mistrust.
That we could wake tomorrow
with the world's enormous sadness gone
and the garden cleansed to innocence; the apple
luminous and whole upon the branch,
never bitten.

# The Children Beckon, Late

Dense with sleep
and thick with midnight hibernation,
they lumber to my bed at 4:00 a.m.

Little bear cubs, winter's almost thawed.
I can shelter you from nightmare,
wrap you in the starry folds

of my blue mother-quilt,
but only for a time.
When adulthood summons,

you'll forget the hundred backrubs
that soothed a child's deep panic,
and that will be all right.

Other women will hold you, measure
the grown male fears of you,
and gently draw you from the cave

to springtime's light.
I wish these women grace and courage
now, as I meet another sleepless night.

# Under It All

The locked beauty of my sons in sleep:
they swim transparent there, unburdened
by the weight of gender and its deep
divides, that mass of land they can't transcend.
The last words they used on me tonight
were their supreme insult: "You're a *girl*,
Mom, and that's it." Called to fight,
I fought the urge to strangle or to whirl
them senseless on the bed and stopped
before the Ninja-turtle instinct summoned reason
clean away. Then Naoise yawned and swore
he wanted just one kiss. I thought of men
and boys, and wept. I thought of all of this,
and mourned my dolphins' hidden gentleness.

# All is Calm, All is Bright

*for Naoise, Conor and Brian*

Praise the tree, the cranberry-popcorn garlands
strung after dinners in December,
my small boy-terrorists' conversion
to positive reflection.  Sing its "ancient"
pre-school ornaments, each happy yelp
of recognition by those boys.  Let our new
guinea pig, Spooky, roam freely on the floor
among pine needles, and Radio Ahhs play
"O Christmas Tree" once more.  That star
that Naoise climbed the couch and window-sill
to crown the tree with—let it bless our house
with faith and reverence for birthdays
bigger than Santa Claus.  And when
the world's armaments grow silent
for their annual truce, when all the lights
are out except the white bulbs circling
the midnight crèche, let me stop to celebrate
those boys in anxious sleep upstairs and send
a silent wish to that other child I love,
sleeping in St. Paul.  As grace abounds tonight
and magic hums its low background song,
I'll climb the stairs in grateful prayer
for every spark of love that lives.

# Long Distance

Time rushes backward through the wires—
their voices on the phone tonight small
as early childhood, reeling me back
to Naoise with peas stuck in his ears, to Conor
in that store hissing to the kind clerk
that God *gave* him that truck,
so bug off.  Hanging up, I thought of the kid
this morning doing handstands
on the lawn, how I wanted to grab the bright coin
of him and squander its riches all on me
until love and poverty were the only things left.

We always want what's leaving us:
our sons like meteors, speeding away
from us toward adolescence;
that moment in October when light
charges leaves and limbs equally
and then vanishes; the song
whose words slip away in sleep,
troubling our morning coffee.

Talk to me, babies, rub the ocean's joy
into the mouthpiece until I feel the salt
on your lips as you answer me
in monosyllables, *nope, yep, 'K, bye,*
holding back the thing
you don't know how to give.

# Mother/Son

His room is adolescent male, his own
retreat against the gust of female light
his mother casts around him.  He can't remember
that she knew him first as body
of her own body, swimming dark
inside her like a fish, first son.

Years she marveled at his flesh, this son.
There were no boundaries to divide his own
skin from hers; even in the dark
night of nursing they were one light
rocking by the window, one body.
This sense of peace is something she remembers.

He tires of her repetitions: *remember*
*your homework, remember the trash.*  What son
wouldn't?  The way she hovers over, a body
couldn't breathe.  He'd die to make his own
life far away from her, to light
the house on fire and run into the dark

where no one knew him as a child, the dark
house in flames, a dream he can't remember.
He studies his legs in the bath, the curls of light
hair sprouting reward for any son
along with height and Adam's apple, his own
fierce trophies, these changes of the body.

She loves his colt-like awkwardness, his body
lurching upward overnight from dark;
the way the Dodgers baseball cap he owns
is angled backward.  She remembers
him minutes old; how foreign now, this son
who hides from her and turns away from light.

Headphones on, he turns off the light.
The bed's a little short for his body.
He gathers what he knows as firstborn son
around him, unravels into dark
and sleep, trying hard to remember
what part of him is hers and what's his own.

She surrenders him, her son, the dark
night's body shielding what each owns.
Years from now, they'll each remember light.

# Déora Dé

*for my father*

We walked through a tunnel of fuchsia
and he called the bushes *Déora Dé.*
"From the Irish," he said, *Tears of God.*
How like him it was to pull his other language
from the air like that,

threading the red blaze of color
and its teardrop song to the sorrow spent
by one creating it, petal by detailed petal
added to a burden of immense particulars
in a world still daily being made.

My father—his thin shoulders angling
through the patched tweed jacket,
our hands linked by the old stories,
fused history cast in common bone.
And the wild fuchsia light
on the West Cork mountains
that October afternoon.

# Dinner at the Frost Place

*for Susan Roney O'Brien*

Brazilian music and the slow sax
of Stan Getz steaming in the kitchen
to the pulse of simmering garlic.
Sweet zucchini sheds its speckled skin
in Susan's sauce and Elizabeth sambas slowly
across the floor, five men in a trance
behind her.  We have cast a spell on anyone
who enters here tonight, three women
armed with poetry and the charm of food.
Our arugula lies succulent and tender
around the bed of wet cucumbers
and red tomatoes, our eggplant swells
with mozzarella in the oven, our sauce
gains velocity as it heats.  We sway
to this summer music with loose hips
and sweaty cheeks, our cooking spoons
raised like wands.  Such ripeness!
And now the wine, a gentle red fire
in the stomach.......come moon-light,
bread nearly flies from the oven
and *The Girl From Ipanema* throws away
her combs.  None of us has ever known
such lyric food, such bardic guests,
such high July happiness before.

# Chamomile

This morning walking the usual trail
I noticed chamomile, its pale root
tapered as a mouse-tail entering the dirt,
the green nub of its flower spiked
with a halo of yellow hairs, a furry aureole.
Crushing the warm bulb between my thumb
and finger I inhaled the future scent
of steeping tea from mashed, dried greens.
And I thought of its power to soothe
the nightmares from a child's brow,
to slow the racing heart of the man on death row,
to calm the earth's tilt, even for just
a millisecond. I almost missed it,
common weed among the scrubgrass—
the sheer tenacity it owns
in springing back when walked on, the secrets
packed in the heart of its densely woven bud.

# In Time

Everything reveals itself in time.
I simply counsel patience when I feel
your soul alive like this so close to mine.

Inside its shell the oyster sleeps in brine,
its hidden pearl glowing and surreal.
Everything reveals itself in time.

In April tulip hearts begin their climb
from earth to light; the world starts to heal.
Your soul's alive like this so close to mine.

We work to unlock mysteries and find
our palms raw and empty, so we kneel.
Everything reveals itself in time.

Come evening, stars tumble, then align
themselves in constellation.  Can they anneal
your soul, alive like this, so close to mine?

Much effort makes the perfect rhyme
and waiting has its worth, its own appeal.
Everything reveals itself in time,
your soul alive like this so close to mine.

# Driving the Coast Road to Dingle

*for John Sweetser 1919-1998*

The light was thinning.  Dusk fell
in soft haphazard clumps on the sheep,
the hills, the long streak of sea
below, the boys sprawled across
the back seat, their smell of wet wool,
of child-musk and sleep.

Ahead, two horse-trailers took the curves
slow and their brake-lights deepened
on-off, on-off, a red glow.  Who
could hear me singing on this road
above the sea, who could hear
the leaps and dives my heart made
on-off, on-off, as I drove?

We headed west into dark
toward the harbour-town
whose name repeated in my brain
like rain sweeping now
across the windshield.  The Volvo
skimmed hedge rows to the left
and my hands gripped the steering wheel
a few times before the boys woke up.

At that moment
stars began to push
their white necks through
the shawled sky above.
I knew then there was no
inch of earth, no
other world than this
I loved.

# Three Wishes for Brian

That
you know your belovedness
to each mother

Whom you own;
to the father who claimed you
as a falling star

Prized
among multitudes
of hot silver;

To your brothers
who have high-fived
the toddler-photo of you

Holding a fish
for years now   as they've passed it
on the refrigerator door.

Child
of my heart, how you've grown
into your long-stemmed body!

Four-and-a-half-years
tall, five years later, your
glad spirit

Bells, bends
each of our lives with music
I can at last and only

Call joy.

# At This Moment

And if I have nothing to say
and all the words inside my brain
are hollowed out, scraped clean, gone,
then let nothingness stream forth
in rows of blazing zeroes.
Let emptiness be the still lake it is
where I coast in my small boat
fishing for the thing I cannot find,
the lake where stones travel
searching lifetimes for the bottom.
Let silence come like animals
in the dark mountain night,
watchful yet unafraid, licking my body
with tenderness the way a mother bear
licks her cubs, less to clean them
than to give them strength.
Let the absent words dissolve
before they're formed
and the fret and strain of pulling
one sentence toward the next
slacken, until all that's left
is something wild and musical,
one note without speech.

# Homage to the Common

How I love the blazing dailyness
of this world, the way my shoes
wear down their heels in the same spot
each year; the gene-print of freckles
on my children's cheeks, the plain truth
that dust-balls breed, regardless;
the unmade beds and other signs
of absent domesticity, the late-night hum
of the furnace pumping out its heat,
even the knots in my shoulders
I've known since childhood.

I celebrate alike the lumpy August lawn
awash with acorns and the first new snow
which tempers any memory of wrong;
my aging Ford Escort and the slush
that city buses sling across its windshield,
the pageantry of light each morning
from the east, strong coffee
halved by cream; that in these last late years
of the 20th century, this planet
keeps on spinning toward some destiny
beyond our knowing.  And always,

how utterly my friends astonish me
with their simple ordinary faith and care
for this or that.  For the common grace
of all of it, the way the earth's
relentless lovely roots pull us deeper
in, I offer blessings, praise,
amazement.

*from*

# Sky Thick With Fireflies

(Salmon Poetry, 2011)

# Birthmother to Her Sleeve

I've lost you since the day that you began.
Small spark begun as love, you changed
to inconvenience as you grew, your kinsman
father running toward the exit as arranged.

Small spark begun as love, you changed
from infant into boy.  Great joy
you brought another family as arranged,
black grief I knew like Troy.

From infant into boy you caused great joy
for someone else.  Not me.  I missed you always
in the black grief I knew like Troy;
ruined, I unlearned the verb *to pray*.

For someone else, not me, you bloomed always,
no inconvenience as you grew, your kinsman
father ignorant of the verb *to pray*.
I've lost you since the day that you began.

# July 4th, Late

Late now, and rain flays the lake
like stones drilling holes in black glass.
His absence like a phantom limb, I break.

My older children sleep.  For whose sake
do they keep one foot in childhood, what task?
Late now, rain flays the lake.

Across the water, fireworks.  They take
me straight to terror, things vanishing, the past
an absence like a phantom limb.  I break.

Can any child simply be mistake?
I take out my grief and polish its sorry brass.
Late now, rain flays the lake.

Like stars, the lights dazzle and leave, opaque
as morning fog rising now from grass.
His absence like a phantom limb, I break.

Can sun take the morning, remake
its torn edges into something seamless?
Late now, rain flays the lake.
His absence like a phantom limb, I break.

# Falling

All day I'd been skidding
toward the thin rim of despair, teetering
like the circus acrobat
who goes on anyway, the net gone.
There are moments to jump, I know that;
reasons to enter the fire and walk out cleansed,
just as times it's necessary
to seize the air like rope and not let go.

I felt raw—the wind bit at my skin,
every birdsong was wrong, my throat
harbored sand and fishbones,
purple lupines hurt me with their deep indifference
and their beauty, someone's death pressed
against my left shoulder, and I knew that
sorrow was feeding her horses again,
preparing the journey down.

I remembered the Jonestown dreams
I couldn't lose for months and the burn
on Conor's hand as he reached
for balance but grabbed instead the barbecue stand.
I remembered the flat tone war in Belfast took in time
as each day's gestures emptied to the next.
And I thought of the indigo of Devin's eyes
when he was born, how when he left my arms
two days later for another mother
that blue was the one raft I clung to.

Tell me how to unlearn fear—
how to tame the horse's bared eyes
and teeth until they're friends to me,
safe as my lover's hands. Tell me how to ride that horse
like my twin; how to plunge my feet
into his sides while we braid our own coarse hair
together to become one animal
at peace with falling.

# Narcissus at the Pond

I bent down,
my face so close
it grazed the surface
of the water.
My kingdoms hovered
above, below,
and a slight breeze
blew ripples of light
that quaked as the wind
rowed them toward me.

How I loved
what I saw!
Cloud-journeys,
a hummingbird's
red whir, the long arms
of the tree limb,
its black fingers
darkening the stones
below the water's seam,
the whole world
given twice.

The same moment
that I saw the world
that lived *on* water
I knew also
what lay below:
the fluid slipperiness
and teeth of fish,
the softness
of moss-covered wood
and pebble, every
aching hue my own.

And when
I raised my head
a few inches
*he* appeared,

his face swaying
and breaking apart
from its own beauty,
luminous.  I touched
his cheek with my thumb
and he felt the weight
of my love for him,
his face shifting
to a dozen gorgeous faces
all at once.
Like an animal in fright,
completely still,
I held my breath
until he reappeared.

Sick with longing,
I think of him tonight,
like all nights, like all
days. To apprehend
such beauty and never
have it apprehend me—
to watch what I love
disintegrate from my touch—

I went back to the pond
in the winter and though
I rubbed the blurred ice
until a lighter circle formed,
I could not make him reappear.

Now the lilac's heady smell
has called me back again,
the ice gone, the water clear and sweet.
He was there. I didn't dare move
except to whisper of my passion…
*Oh, my gazelle, my one*
*sky, my only glass*
*of ruby wine, how I love you!*

His mouth
echoed the same words,
his lips moved exactly
as my own lips
moved, almost like a mirror.

And when I looked down
the last time,
he was crying, too.

# Scissors

I always know where they're put away
in the kitchen drawer, though
I've left them sometimes on the floor
for days, abandoned next to tape and glue,
stars and paper, someone's project for school.
I love their light rasp when opened,
the tune they make when clicking shut.
What lives they've lived inside my hands,
those angled bows of orange plastic,
their gun-metal legs pointed below.
What witness they've borne to my journey,
the first to feel my braids falling
from my shoulders when I cut them
cleanly as my childhood at thirteen.
Such comfort that their snug fit provides
when slicing into new fabric
for a new dress, a new life; how helpful,
tonight, their blades, as I shred to bits
old letters, photographs,
every trace of the unwanted past.

# Third Elegy

I miss you, Stephen, even now, decades
past the day you let the gun release
its last retort into your head.
Imagining your blond hair white
today, the flesh beneath your neck slack
and jowly, your imagination slowed
from manic to considered like a meteor
on lithium, I would still prefer
the fire absent from your eyes than
your absence.  Old companion,
how the world diminished afterward
in places where you walked and shook
the seventies to dizzy bits
along the Mississippi water-flats
and streets of Minneapolis!
Tonight, this new and shaky century,
shakier somehow without you:
a bell is tolling *wrong, wrong, wrong.*

# Jeff's Poem

*for the Fridlunds, and for all of us*

Once, the steady burning of a sturdy star,
golden, prime, bright.
Then darkness and the enormous wheel
of absence, the reeling weight of it
too much to hold.  Then numbness,
the necessary blur of motion,
anything to fill his place: impossible.

At Christmas the tree went up.  Maybe
the Vikings lost; it didn't matter.
By spring the world bloomed relentlessly
as usual, surge of blossom, heady earth.
We kept remembering, kept walking,
one foot shepherding the next stumble.

A shift, come summer, all our longing
pulled to something tangible
that said his name: *Jeff*.  And it became
the father, *raise high the roofbeams,
carpenter*, as he constructed a gazebo.
And it became the mother, cutting pavers
for the garden on a brick-saw with a diamond tip,
measuring, shoveling Class 5 pebbles, sand and dirt;
and loosening, letting go, as spirit
grew around her.

And it became sister, brother,
wielding hammers
and remembering Jeffrey as they laughed
and bossed the crew.

And it became the aunts
who'd watched Jeffrey grow
and mourned him as their own, adding
their sweat to the earth and stone—

and the uncles both here and elsewhere,
each, too, a part of this.
And it became a slight dark-haired girl
who held herself sometimes
because she'd watched her first love
die, but circling now, intent, around pink star-gazer lilies
with her watering can, an orange monarch
butterfly behind her.

And it became the gardener-healer
and her husband, who planned an arc
of luminous foliage framing that gazebo, so lovely
in their dirt-stained clothes they shone
as deeply as those shrubs and flowers.

And it became a stranger
who became their friend, the shy brick-layer
who never knew their son.

And it became Jeffrey, intelligent,
silent, lion-hearted, present everywhere around us,
examining the yellow light of the azalea,
the deep green yew and purple salvias,
dappled strands of the willow's spreading arms.

And it became all of us, a community of love
large enough to exile loss a few mountains west
for a few minutes or a few months;
small enough to hear Jeffrey's voice there
with us, roots in his family, laughing
as he walked with his God.

# Eastern Standard Time 9-11-01

*for my NYC Irish-born grandparents*

In Dublin it is nearly four o'clock
and O'Connell Street is thick
with traffic.  School-children throng
the buses home and shoppers exit
Cleary's, pleased with bargains.

Turn the clock back to Eastern time,
New York, 10:00 a.m.  The sky rains
high-heeled shoes and light
flaming bodies; ash, chalk, dust,
bone, the grit of ruined things.

Sirens wail from Maine to Iowa
and on CNN, the Twin Towers explode
again and yet again.  Grief
goes off like landmines, unexpectedly,
the woman watching TV stunned by pain.

My Irish cousins gather by the phone
in Donnybrook and Harold's Cross
as evening spreads slow from Dublin mountains,
a dropping of purple, the murmur of rhymes
recited at bedtime, September's long song.

Across the sea, the waiting dead assemble
patiently, knowing they cannot rest
until they're found.  Days slide
to weeks; their bodies sway with fatigue.
*Margaret, kiss the boys for me.*

Numbness. A metallic taste.
The world tilted sideways. The papers
fatten with obituaries,
"Loved to Cook," "Family Man,"
"Sorely Missed by Wife and Son."

# What's Said

Everything I just told you was a lie.
The small domesticities of tenderness
in the kitchen, the village where my grandmother
was born, how I only drink socially,
even the angle of light on my child's face
in sleep, a lie.

Nothing ever is as it appears: remember that
as you invent the shade of paint needed
to construct beautiful artifice, or fall
so deeply for the characters in your novel
you disconnect the phone to hold
the long conversation in the living room.

Your teenage daughter smoothes the dent
of her boyfriend's frame from the bed
before you wake, saying nothing;
the body count in the war contains
fabrications; rain's predicted
but it snows; you say "I'm fine, I'm really *fine*
when you aren't, and somewhere
in between lies a fraction of the truth.

# Brother of Music

I am in love with the voice
of a man who lives down the street.
Cutting through my lawn at night
he sings an old Righteous Brothers tune
*a capella* as he wanders home:
*"Oh, my love, my darling,*
*I hunger for your touch..."*

And the timbre of his notes
clings to kitchen curtains blowing
in the breeze, sets the bedroom rug fur
on end, lays a restless spell
on my twisted summer sheets.
*"But time goes by so slowly,*
*and time can mean so much—*
*are you still mine?"*

August thunder hums, then hesitates
as his clear voice blends with rain
in the darkness at the end of our block.
*"The long lonely years..."*
A sweet tenor, deep alto
cradling my ears, steaming my bones
like the comfort of hot towels

in a winter without heat
and I want, I want, I want
to whisper from the window
*"don't go—"*
God speed your love, wherever,
and goodnight, brother.

# The Men in the Basement

The men in the basement are tired,
they say, of working without a contract.
I've heard their low grumbles in the evenings
as I read by the stove, and the word union
has slipped through the floorboards once or twice.

It was easier when there was just one—
mild, handsome Jake who fixed the faucets
when they leaked, bled the radiator pipes in Fall,
hung paintings on the bedroom walls
and was happy with a plain pork chop dinner,
desserts a few nights a week.

Then Ted knocked one night, his bag of metaphors
slung on one shoulder, the whole bright alphabet
spilling on the threshold. Because the house repairs
were caught up and because the poem
I was working on was a little bare, I let him in.
We talked till dawn in the kitchen, and I swore
I'd only borrow what I needed from his bag,
then made another bed up in the basement.

These days it seems a little servicing
will only go so far. The philosopher complains
I no longer help him wring meaning
from the stars, the accountant disapproves
of the red ink in my books, and my handyman
threatened to move on today when he found
the poet in my bed tucking images inside my pillow.

The trouble with fantasies is that
they become unwieldy, swelling into great,
lumbering bears with large paws
who outgrow their downstairs beds
and begin to roar for more food, more
attention, more me. I hate to add
a locksmith to the mix, but
I need one for that basement door.

# Loss: An Inventory in Chorus

I lost my shoes and shirt last night,
sleeping at that big downtown shelter
where bodies sprawl mat-to-mat
in the hundreds.  I'd used the shirt & shoes
as my pillow; when I woke,
my head was on the floor.

I'd been doubled up at Jenna's for a month, sleeping
on the couch.  When the fire came there wasn't time
to find Anna's baby photos or the one copy of my
resume on disk. *Start again, my friend*; that old refrain
I'd come to hate.

I've never lost my vodka bottle
but cell phones?  I've lost my share.
The current one is missing
with links to anyone who mattered
and now I think I'll lose my mind.

> What I can carry is a bedroll
> and a few plastic bags.
> The apartment is a memory, those dishes
> with a swirl of cherries on the edge,
> the green velvet couch, my ID
> and birth certificate filed who-knows-where.

I've lost my case manager, she either quit
or traded me for someone else.

> I've lost two toes to frostbite,
> my front teeth to a fight, my girlfriend
> to alcohol, my dog tags to a hole
> in the frayed pocket of a jacket.

Some nights I feel I've lost the dead,
my mother who would come to me in dreams,
her long black hair braided with softest feathers,
the small sun-catcher spilling light
at her throat.  Gone now, the dreams;
bow to the streets, our future king.

# Shelter

*Lottery*

No one talks much during lottery,
all eyes on the Bingo balls
placed in the bowl.  I write the numbers
by each man's name on the list.
The names of the men stand for beds,
or the desire for one.  Who will win?
There are five spaces here
and three referral slots at Our Savior's.
But there are forty-seven men, and this means
some will get the tramp camp downtown
and sleep badly as they guard their shoes,
some will lay their bodies down outside
under the freeway bridge nearby, and some
will drink Nyquil in the alley until dawn.


*Invisible, Among the Men*

When Ramon clips his toenails
at the chair beside our table and Tim
scratches his huge belly
above the too-small, on-loan sweatpants
he wears while his clothes spin
in the dryer, I know I am invisible,
a volunteer, another night attendant.
These men are going about their business,
showering and rubbing powder
into athlete's foot, pulling off
their jeans to lounge in boxers,
rearranging their bundled bags
carefully. I look at the floor,
pretend I'm the Thursday nurse
in a boarding school in England,
my long dress and starched cap
blending with the walls.

*Cigarette Break*

I could smoke all night with them,
Manuel of the clean pressed pants
who thinks I'm from the INS, Manuel
of the earned paranoia; and Billy,
who tells me of the house he owned
two mortgages ago, the repossessed truck
he believes a bankruptcy lawyer
could help him get back. I hand Mike one,
then Lamont, and they're amazed I smoke
at all, much less two brands. I tell them
my story about hedging bets with death,
how when I turned thirty I bought Camel Lights
and tried to alternate with Marlboros,
how I really didn't use the word *death*
to myself but *mortality* instead
because it felt a little vaguer. I light one
more because we all have time on our hands,
because my ten-year-old is at his dad's
tonight where he is building a house
under the blanket for his cat, tucking her in
snug; where he will fall asleep holding
what he loves, knowing, even deep in childhood,
there is no greater shelter.


*Remembering Luxembourg*

The other volunteers don't sleep
well here either. Tonight
I lie awake remembering Luxembourg,
the train station where travelers
could pay to bathe after nights of sleeping rough,
how I put my coins in the slot and felt
such gratitude for water and for soap
that I walked two miles to that small cathedral
on the postcard to think about it all.

Light slanted through stained-glass,
turning the hair on my arms gold.
I remember this: thumb out in the rain
hours later, heading to Switzerland,
I was still warm.


*Order*

I love the supplies closet, tidiest
of anything here with its rows
of fragrant soap in boxes, bowls
of bright packaged condoms
laid out like mints after dinner,
little sample-size shampoos
and rolls and rolls of toilet paper.
The way the tubes of toothpaste
line up back to back and the razors lie
sharp-side down in their plastic clips
soothes me after what happened
earlier, Kevin screaming
as the paramedics held him down
on the stretcher while they filled a vein
in his arm with Valium
before driving him away.


*Refuge*

What I know about shelter
is this: nights I've wanted
to phone a friend to ask
for safety, quick, quick, asylum
please, before I lost it all.  Some days
I've even had to hide the bullets in the freezer
from myself.  Don't tell me shelter
doesn't have arms, substance,
residue.  I've been without.
And tasted it.

*4:00 a.m.*

When there is no light but the gold grid
of stars from the storage closet
patterned on the stained floor,
and no sound but an industrial hum
from the smoke-fan in the hallway
and the quiet turnings of sleeping men
dreaming, perhaps, of their mothers
before turning off the light, or else dreaming
of a different woman reaching for them
once, with love, then it is time for me to wake Miguel
for the long bus ride to his morning shift
in the suburbs, to lay out the Cheerios
and milk on the table and wheel the great vat
of coffee from the kitchen to the hall.

# Dear God of H_____

Oh God of the trumpet red sunrise
burning through the tarp above my tent;
dear God of the warming jeans on the clothesline
hooked between two trees,
God of Dan's sleeping form, let him wake
and light the fire for coffee, let him not
be too hungover from dreams of Gulf War fires
or from vodka; let peace roll over our small camp
as it deserves to roll.

Lord of Shelterdom, I've been to your floor mats
on Currie Avenue, I've watched
more crack pipes brighten up the street
than the bored security officers have seen;
I've had my shoes stripped from me in the night
and have been punched when brushing past another man's mat
while getting up to use the john. Lord, I've entered
your chapel of the Salvation Army and felt no salvation there
where I've almost spit, God, on *you*, my God on you.

Yahweh of joblessness, when the plant closed
the kids and I became a rudderless boat
careening through deepening waves.
Jonah hates the "shelterbus" ride to school; Jane's too young
to know.  Today I walked to Welfare to complete more forms,
then to a market two miles away for dinner things, then
to the diabetes clinic for my check-up.  My feet burn,
my toes are fat cows.  Holiness, I have no busfare.

Rain down, oh rain down, you desolate
blessed God of homelessness.
You with your large hands,
play it out: bestow on us every clement bit of justice
that you own, for today is a day tender as April,
and it carries the shudder of goodness.

# Fireflies

Surge and dim, the fireflies
say, here is our light,
our brief hum; look twice,
we're gone.

I remember the sky thick
with them in childhood,
their soft throb of yellow
glowing above the barn
where the woods begin.
My father helps me
catch them, one small spark
at a time.  We cup a lid
on their fire in the jar,
then I take the wealth
inside, but the airholes
aren't big enough
and in the morning
they're dead bugs
again. My dad nods,
he's seen it before.

*What made me think*
*I could keep fire?*
*What made me think*
*I could keep anything,*
*much less desire?*

Now my father's head
is being mapped for radiation,
lines drawn across his throat,
a helmet fitted to his skull
to chart the space of flesh
the doctors want to burn.
Little errant cells have hid
before the surgeon's scalpel
and have migrated now

to a distant lymph node
to begin another life.
The light of a man
dimming.  The tall pine
my father was, the fire in him
bright as fireflies blinking and hiding
and blinking their brilliance again
inside green-needled limbs.
Now his grey branches
stoop with snow, all the sparks
asleep, breezing away
so gently by degrees through the night,
fire blown to the winds.

# The Scholar in the Playroom

My father's head was propped up in his hands.
Around him chaos swirled; the cello played
off-key in practice, someone vacuumed sand
we'd tracked in from the beach.  I was amazed

that he could concentrate through all of this,
scoring Shakespeare's words with yellow pen
and calmly reading as I wrestled Fergus
while the youngest blundered through the den.

For years I've carried my father's image around,
the flame in the storm who loved the crazy wind
his children were despite the din of sound
he sometimes wished he could rescind.

He proved the ivory tower a myth, this anti-Lear,
who kept his children, his Cordelias near.

# Nothing Gold

Everything my father's loved is leaving—
the taste of whipped cream dessert
at lunch; the bloom of Russian sage
in the August garden; the words
to his beloved Emily's poems;
that Irish tune my mother used to hum.

Tonight he thinks he is a prisoner, poisoned
by my older sisters, whose names he can't recall.
On the telephone he sounds afraid and frail.
Voice low, he asks when I can come to get him, do I know
the street number of the house where he is being held,
how soon, God help us, can I get there?

And I am desperate not to hear this story, wild
to seize him from the place where his brain flares
and slows, just as his gait, too, has slowed
to shaky, baby steps that inch their way
out to the car in the driveway.

Mind back, he whispers to me
*"Nothing gold can stay,"* and I recall him
quoting Frost or Yeats at the dinner table
for his nine children through the years,
recall how poems lived in the house
in all the rooms my father walked.
*So dawn goes down to day...*

And oh my father, at this moment
I would welcome the wolves
from that fairy tale you used to tell,
would gladly let the day end with you
tucked upon their sled
headed toward the dark woods—
oh, I'd believe all their promises to take care
of you, I'd believe anything they said.

# Because of Them

Before words had formed
beneath the pulsing fontanels
on their infant skulls,
during the years they slept
through damp-haired Julys
and two-blanket Decembers,
through nights & nights of *please Mom,*
*one more story* and later, the yawning length
of *Tom Sawyer* and *Harry Potter* aloud;
before the blonde girls with restless eyes
began to call, while my sons' bodies
lengthened in their beds as they slept
and their faces changed from boys
at night to men at dawn—
men who spoke the sudden secret tongue
of new initiates, laconic monosyllables
and the speech of turned shoulders—
all this time I went about my life
and cast my nets into the future;
my mother-threads invisible
but sewn lightly to their shoulders
for a time when they might turn
to tug those threads and I would heed the pull,
I would reach backward to the moment
before I even knew their names, I would leave
everything and come to them.

# Ghazal

Say your kisses are small fires on the hillside
of my throat.  All night the flames, the heat, the light.

This morning sun seized the mountain by degrees,
spreading neck to feet its lusty jewelry of light.

Your body underwater in the clear-bottomed lake
stuns me as it loops through scallops of electric light.

The hummingbird just now, stopped in its own air-current.
Before any touch, a blurred vision, a hovering of light.

Trace the imprint of the snail fossilized in stone, the whorls
frozen, and know the heart petrified, deprived of light.

I want to know what print your tongue will make on mine,
what new alphabet desire might create, its weight, its light,

And why speech becomes a useless coin, a kind of poverty
when you enter me, that note of high-pitched singing light.

An unbearable geography, this land of longing; the tension
of a song trapped in stone.  Blaze, stone, then liquefy to light.

Even in the uterus before birth I *knew*—
I saw the verge of egg and sperm exploding into light

and wanted nothing more than this: to follow it, your kiss upon my throat.
Dear God, I swear I've spent my *lifetime* being faithful to this light.

# Swannanoa Afternoon

*for Eleanor Wilner*

Under the vine-cloaked trees
a June wind rains down orphaned leaves,
pin-oak and palm-sized maple,
scraps of locust.  Through the slats

of the bench where I sit, ivy sinews
upward, lacing a pattern of new green
against the weathered old.  I'm in that idle
weightless state of watching everything

and watching nothing, thinking at once
of my dead parents, of the bee hovering
near my foot, the vagaries of solitude
and the far drone of cars on the mountain road,

of that time I told my youngest child
that love was worth risking everything
and then lived my days in careful distance
from that declaration.

A ladybug alights on my wrist,
deliberate, speckled, beautiful.
It is so peaceful here alone,
the blurred croak and hum of bullfrogs

by the pond, birdsong
layering the air in different keys.
Now the lemon finch I've been tracking
lands nearby, then ascends; shreds

of a nest-in-the-making drifting from its beak.
I reach and finger what the bird has left me,
hold its difficult weight of goldenness, of dun.
Oh irony, the flattened years when

I expected nothing—then this slow tilt
toward meaning in the small.
*Move*, the bird seems to urge.
And I do.

*from*

# Swimming With Shadows

(Salmon Poetry, 2019)

# Storm, Lake Superior

If ever I were to fall in love
again, it's likely not
to be with someone human,
but with a moment just like this one—

a lit expanse of water during storm
forked by lightning from sky to lake,
some crazed color between silver and white—
light flashing staccato below a grey band

of clouds, waves that bluster in
while wind billows and thunder rumbles
deep.  There I'd know a hum
of both aloneness and connection,

sky brilliant and alive, stars electric
after rain, the aftermath of storm
searing through my brain
with a depth I've never known.

# Thanks

What to praise but the ordinary—
the ant burrowing in sidewalk sand,
kitchen faucet that no longer drips,
pink bee balm from the garden
fringed like spiky fireworks,
all the words on the page of this book,
the halleluiah clouds floating in today's sky,
that sharp garlic smell wafting from the pan,
red postage stamps with jazz notes and poets,
the eagle's nest on my street by the river,
a pealing laugh heard anywhere;
your arms, which once circled mine
in benign sleep; the sunrise that beckons us
to wake daily and begin again.

# Abandon

As in to let go utterly,
the highest gold leaf diving
from the maple tree.  Or that first time
on the beach under stars, terrified
by raw tenderness, by depth.
I saw a firefighter today
blaze into a building not worth
saving and I said a prayer—
God, let me lose any kinship
to the inconsequential
when it's my turn to dive
without the parachute.
When I become the highest leaf
in the sky, grace me
with pure abandon.

# Our Ancestral Ghosts

The tall shadow from the roof at Sheeaun
forms a dark vee across the lawn lit with stars
behind the house belonging to my brother Fergus.
Calm settles like a sigh upon the town below,
and a low wind forms a scrim
upon the surface of Lough Derg
a half mile beneath the house.

I have come to see the yellow gorse
of County Clare where my grandmother
was born, the rocky landscape past
the Burren that leads straight to the sea,
the fuchsia-studded, foxglove-dusted hills
she walked before she left for New York.

Look, see how this house holds
a part of her, holds my brother's fiddle music
as it echoes through the kitchen at Sheeaun
each night, reaching back from the future
to her ears while she stands and stares at the sea,
humming to herself a forward tune; see how
we hold our ghosts of history dear.

# The FBI / Klan Murders, 1963

*for Faith & the rest, especially those no longer living*

We were thirteen
or maybe we were twenty-three; it didn't matter.
We each read the papers on that Sunday
morning, sitting in the heart
of American living rooms.

*I pledged allegiance to the flag*

We were no different from the rest.
Bred from the cradle on a hopeful legacy,
we took our proper shapes; dreamed
the speeches of freedom while fed on the fire

*of the United States of America*

of shots heard round the world.  But this, now,
this is the wear on the edge of the star,
the worm surfacing in the best fruit—
How I have wanted to burn all the books

*and to the Republic for which it stood*

that lied to me, how I was too young
to know what fire meant
in Birmingham to four small girls
my age; how that newsprint made our eyes
blur, and the tremor in my pulse
made my fixed wrists ache.

*one nation; where was God?*

I want them to know
that the air in every room
was tarnished by lies, that we were afraid
to sleep at night; that there is danger
in language and it was even perilous
to read each other's eyes.

*indivisible, with liberty and justice for some.*

# Dumpster

And that was their home for three days
of our most bitter winter in decades,
a dozen bags of garbage
buffering the beast of cold iron
burning at their sides.
At daybreak they left
for the hour-long coffee sipped at Denny's,
then the library, warm,
where she played Solitaire
as he searched on Craigslist once again
for jobs.  Later, a bus ride to the terminal
and back on the 16A for a nap.
Come evening
dread raised its whip again,
*can't do it no more.*
But they did, and that's where
I found them, frostbitten in the alley,
huddled in that dumpster in a world
gone raw, curdled, wrong.

# Wind Song

*for Tammie, 1970-2014*

Cheap, heady, the perfume of my youth
or maybe my older sister's,
along with *White Shoulders* and *Chantilly*.
Half the boys of my generation
kissed necks scented with *Wind Song*
before they left for Vietnam.

And now at the Dollar Store, Tammie
snatches a 99-cent *Wind Song* knockoff
and sprays it on her wrist, the only perfume
she can afford.  We each breathe deep,
her homelessness obliterated by the smell
that hits endorphins in our brain cells,
that sensual leap into our separate histories.

Let's pretend Tammie doesn't live
on the streets or seek men for shelter
each night to survive.  Pretend instead that crack
hadn't ruined the spark in those eyes
or worn down that fierce spunk she owned.

Imagine for a moment she wears
sapphire earrings, her dress
a black line of elegance,
her wrists, her neck wafting
*Wind Song* as she walks airily.
Pretend before she overdosed at 44,
she knew the deep rock-peace
of someone loving her.

# After the Election

*"Nothing like a little disaster to sort things out"*

Heather-Derr Smith

Calamity rocks the scales, catastrophe
destroys them.  After the piano-man arrives,
the fractured ivories are replaced.
No blood-stain of history remains, just
the bright, pale keys awaiting sound.

Who's counting?  One by one they fall,
every liberty we thought we knew
gone—Jill and Georgia's marriage voided
by the state, waterboarding legal once again—
the emperor has no clothes!  And ah,

it hurts.  Disaster clears, cleans the air,
separates the princess from the serf,
divides our joy into grief.
Here it comes with its monstrous knife,
slicing pieces of the only life,

the only earth
we thought we knew.

# Ubuntu

*South African philosophy of interconnectedness,*
*"I am who I am because of who we all are."*

I pick up my child to whom I am connected
but no more own then a leaf on the poplar tree,
a child who could be blown away
with the first October wind
or a semi-automatic in Newtown, Connecticut.

The fierce stars webbed across the sky tonight
are linked in their blaze of necklaced light,
radiant yet plain as that old Irish proverb
drifting through my brain,
*"Ar scáth a chéile a mhaireann na daoine,"*
"It is in the shadow of each other
that the people live."

This morning the news say
that 90 people lined up at a bakery
in Syria have been killed by an airstrike
and in Afghanistan, the task of suicide
achieved its aim.

There is a chink in the chain
where the linkage has been broken
and the missing have wandered out
into the ruined world, searching
for Ubuntu.

# The Summer Poet

Never mind the year-long gruel
of writing line after line
like some bricklayer's job, day in
and out.  I've completed that apprenticeship
already, sweated the construction
of each metaphor, every simile,
packing images like insulation behind drywall,
hoisting rhyme to the roofbeams
as I labored on the difficult house
of poetry.

Now I've become a summer poet,
dwelling in the place where less
is more, where master writers line up eagerly
to drink the sweet concentrate of energy
that produces high-octane poetry in weeks,
guaranteed.  You've seen that ad on TV
I'm describing, right?  So far I like it
well, my new ornate journal full
by noon, the fevered evenings crammed
with delirious poems, the whole intense

compression of it all, like getting
a degree by mail from the divinity school
and presto, Reverend overnight!
I do confess to some weariness after no sleep
in four days, and I find the programmed pen
does indeed cause me to write faster,
harder.  Well—I'll let you know how
it all stacks up when I'm through working
at my summer stint, and which master
that I plan to serve.

# Wednesday at the Frost Place

Poetry sluts, every one of them,
lounging on the porch in pajamas
well after noon, unaware of truck-
drivers' stares as they each strike
the last stanza out and begin again.
Unwashed by noon, Juli's collarbone
slides out her bathrobe as she fills
the margins of her paper till it's black,
nearly missing picking up the ink for a sip.
*("What glazed eyes you have, my dear,"*
said the wolf to the granny.)
Susan lies on her stomach in the grass,
nightgown sailing with the breeze,
studying the geometric lines
of a cobweb with her reading glasses on.
Hours pass.  They are all still slaves
to the pen and the page, this bunch,
the men upstairs sighing in unshaven bliss,
looking like they'd just swallowed light.
From the loom room comes muttering
and promises, the crisp sound
of scissors clipping wasteful words
that clink when they hit the ground.
Money is exchanged, I think, or else
the dedication page to a first book.
Michelle and Betsy hang out the shingle
solemnly: "Editing: the Price is Right."
Of course, it's close to past the picnic time
by now, but who has ever known hunger,
*real hunger* when working on a poem?
Sheila asks herself, minding only slightly
that the crab-cakes will be gone when they arrive.
Now Andrea wanders through.  Dizzy
as a sleepwalker, she repeats a line
that works and then repeats it once again.
Ah, those sluts, those have-to-have-it, outright
poetry sluts.  Give them a day without design
and they'll lie down and lick the shoes
of language, believing that its high buff,
its come-on look exists just for them.

# Monster Kittens

Because they sleep with their small cat-paws
around each other's limbs, and because
they are actual brother and sister with names
dignified as George and Maggie, I have not yet
duct-taped their feet together for smashing plants
in several reckless rampages, nor have I taken
a knife to their tails when they bent the curtain-rod
in half while trying to climb my bedroom curtains.
Dented beyond repair, one rod pressed against
the ceiling, suspended in the air. Let's call them
oh, possessed creatures acting out their calling.
If I can watch them one more time bat the thin spurt
of water falling from the bathroom faucet,
if I can witness their mock-ferocious fighting
as they somersault across the rug, I can sleep,
knowing it's just a matter of time before they lie
in wily, peaceful innocence at the base of my bed.

# The Way Back

And what if I'd gone *this* way
and not that, so many years back?

At the crossroads, two tall glasses,
maybe water, maybe wine.

One stone sings to the other
of its loneliness, and they meet downstream.

Regret's a layered sentiment, shapeshifting
the mountain sideways;

gratitude, contentment, twin flowers
growing upright from bare rocks.

You kissed me, a sear.  I remember
now.  Tang of pine, forest air.

If the meadow is this high today
and this purple, surely you are there?

# Kisses

Lavish were my kisses in my youth,
bright and laughter-filled and free.
A few met their match in heat
and depth; one or two undid me.

So many men I didn't marry;
two I did.  Who knows
whether I'd ever repeat that deed,
but the blessing odds aren't good.

Yet I think I'd still risk another kiss,
chaste at first and full of shy goodwill
before it grew to purpose, before
it grew to longing, before my mouth

was stunned and fevered-full
of hot, swollen want.

But tonight I hid the kiss I didn't give you
inside the box I'd labeled *tenderness*
years back, and placed the small container
in the crevice of my closet wall.

# Lake

Filmy ribs of light
beneath the surface, swirling
as my calves slide in.
Liquid silk immersion, sky above
a calm bowl of blue.
The willow tree on the shore
shaking its arms back and forth.
An oar slap from a boat
far out, then the plunge
underwater, small fish
skittering through a tunnel of arms
that push a breast-stroke forward.
Moonrise through dense trees,
and the certainty
I could swim to Mars.

# Solstice

*for Kathy Jo and Flo*

Embers like small red planets
pulse and glow from the fire-pit
beneath December skies, where
an hour back, flames shot through
the top.  Into the fire we had put
on paper what we most longed to drop
from our lives, and I wrote *the grief
of race and war.*  Then quiet fell,
silent as the horse in a nearby field.

Inside now, every light blazed,
the house lit by friendship
through the long years.
Stars grazed our shoulders
as we ate and talked and ate, then sang.
It was the solstice of our lives,
the new light erasing every wrong
for a moment; the dark river below forgotten.

# Nighttime on the Island

*for Kate Stanley*

And the foghorn a hollow tube
or maybe a calliope breathing its contralto
through the chambers of my inner ear.
And the wind traveling free
through the house, billowing
then slapping this curtain and the next,
blowing toasted bagel crumbs
from the moonlit maple table,
swaying heads of roses in their vases
as it passes.  And the faint tick-tock
of the kitchen clock, and the laundry
on the line perfumed by lavender.
This is the hour of sleep on Martha's Vineyard,
the time when woods behind the house beckon
and thin before dreams begin.

# Leaving

*for Conor*

I turned around tonight to say—

And then I missed you so hard
at that instant, the wry smile of you
absent, every atom of you flown,
not a particle hovering in the house.

I left too, young as you
craving wind-shifts of change,
hitching through Europe in the 70s,
camping rough, picking grapes in France,
bleaching the stain off down in Spain,
five months of glory on the road.

Now the same winds have pushed you
to Mexico, a silver jet seam visible as stars
in the sky last night, that long curl
dissipating into cloud.

Remember how I knew you at five
in that Ninja costume?
I knew you skate-boarding
with an attitude at Brackett Park,
and sensed for certain when
you first fell in love. I knew you
as a heartbeat beneath my ribs
at nine months, almost born.

And know you now,
gone.

# 99 Sheep

I move toward the zone of sleep
but it eludes me.  There are sheep
on the other side, their little baas
and bleats fill the air.  Below
my bedroom window, the scrape
of metal shovel hoisting snow.
Close to midnight now, back and forth
it goes, another irritant in the ether.
Then the wanderings begin—
how do squirrels live till spring,
why is the mind is an elastic thing
that curves memory
until it bends into another form,
where have I put that new tube
of toothpaste, could I hire a hit man
for my supervisor and please,
how far away is Mexico
this long, long winter? Come,
little sheep, lead me home to sleep.

# The Platonic Nap

There are no soft kisses, only
an easiness of arms and legs and backs.
We are both tired, we are friends
from forever, and we each long
to hold the other in sleep.

Every Saturday at 4:00 p.m.
he comes for an hour's rest
in the big bed, his shoulder
against my shoulder, the smell
of man on my arm,
his breath gone slow
and deep with forgetting.

Dreams flip me backward
and I am tossed far from here
to Morocco with my lover in the 70s.
We are young as baby rabbits,
our happiness warms the tiles at our feet
at breakfast, and by noon we mount
the staircase once again
to our room, where it is a tussle
of heat and limbs for hours. No sleep.

You and I? We've climbed the swing bridge
of decades, known our flesh to fail
and humbly rise again, shyly marveled
at each other's freckled hands.
We couldn't be lovers like that,
dear sleeper, dear man,
so we nap the nap of not-sex,
one body warm against the next.

# Turning

And now night lengthens—
the rosy hues spilling on the brick house
next door peak and fade at 4:00 p.m.,
and we leave work with headlights on.
Today was a rare November day
of golden leaves remaining on a few trees,
a sun-filled warmth buffering
my pre-winter dread.

Winter is the season of loss;
every leaf gone from tree,
snow stinging down from clouded sky,
someone slipping on the ice who'll need knee surgery
tonight; a child's frozen mitten flattened
by the weight of tires,
your death, mother, in December
of that coldest year, 1996.

And yet—and yet—despite the dead,
despite light's absence
which bows our heads with longing,
I can't help but know
that hope is my sister
who hovers one step behind me,
and she sings today
of the future, telling me that spring
will come again even as I brave
the cold tunnel of this winter wind.

# Mortal

So earthly, this world,
the three-year-old suddenly a teenager
hurtling toward the future;
those tiny flowers tipped with light
on lilacs, brittled brown
as Fall plows forward;
the lake with its shaky coat
of ice solidifying in a month;
my father's body weightless
as a twig or feather
as he shrinks toward memory.
Who will hold us
in the beautiful world
when everything returns to dust?

# The Need to Sleep

To hide.  Be dead
to what disturbs you when awake.
To crawl into God's immense hands,
the lost sheep come home.
To skim the ache off your bones
with pure inertia,
calm the din in your brain
by entering the cave of dreams.
To stop the ferrets gnawing
at the ribs of your soul.
As rejuvenation, the night-food
necessary for wrestling down
the giants of the morning.
To meet yourself alone
beyond the worst nightmare
and hold one foot firm,
saying "no," utterly not.
To let go deliberately
and lose the trail of breadcrumbs
Hansel left you, walking
headlong into the forest
holding nothing
that you've ever known.

# Afterward, at Lake Superior

*in memory of Brian*

Slate grey, this grief,
made up of rain and whitecaps
and regret; the great lake
swallowing whatever's next.

I could yell his name
all night long
and the roar of waves
would drown each letter.

Dark pines above.  The stars
gone invisible.
A ton of water hurls
itself against the rocks.

This is the last time
I will come here.

# Come Back to the World

Leave the ruined realm
you inhabited those long years,
where bluebirds' song was mute
and oceans never surged
and darkness fell by noon.
Leave your bed and breathe
deep as you run, the sound
of your chest pounding
*yes* in your ears.

Come back to the world.
Learn how to split wood
with a sharpened ax.
Love the new buds
sparking light at ends of branches
in the spring forest; love the yellow gleam
rising from the kitchen floor planks
after being washed.

Love everything, severely and generously
as you'd love yourself.

# Pockets

The way you once sewed loss
like shards of glass
inside the hem of your pockets—
then over time the shards

broke loose, your pockets growing
two miles deep as suddenly
small gratitudes seeped in.
Despite yourself, you felt

the sun's deep heat on freckled arms,
noticed fish in their silver leap
in water, knew you still loved
with the same intensity

you'd always loved, even welcoming
the tempered measure
that diminishes intensity with age.
Come, put it all in those pockets,

in the hems you now know
are bottomless, and walk down
the road open-throated
toward whatever song comes next.

# Publication Acknowledgements

NEW POEMS

"Oh, Maria," *Innisfree Poetry Journal* (Silver Spring, MD), "Light Rolling Slowly Backward," *Days of Clear Light*, Salmon Poetry (Ireland), and "Those Birds I Loved," *Somerset Review* (Smithtown, NY).

*from* CARAVAN

"Speed," *Cyphers* (Dublin, Ireland), "Moving" and "What We Cannot Help," *Milkweed Chronicle* (Minneapolis, MN), "Winter Widower in Key West," *Santa Barbara Independent*, (Santa Barbara, CA), "The Other Woman" and "Going Back," *Unlacing: 10 Irish-American Women Poets* (Fireweed Press, AK), "St. James Orphan," *Open-Eyed, Full-Throated: An Anthology of American-Irish Poets*. Other poems appeared in *Fallout, The Lake Street Review*, and *Northern Lit Quarterly*.

*from* THE ONE WHO SWEARS YOU CAN'T START OVER

"Absences," *Beyond Forgetting: Poetry and Prose About Alzheimer's Disease* (Kent State University Press, Kent, OH), "Potatoes," *Holy! Cow Press* (Duluth, MN), "Homage to the Common" and "At This Moment," *33 Minnesota Poets* (Nodin Press, Minneapolis), and "Driving the Coast Road to Dingle," *The White Page/ An Bhileog Bhán: Twentieth Century Irish Women Poets*, Salmon Poetry (Ireland), "The Otherworld" and "Mountain, the Longing," *The Wild Gods: The Ecstatic in Contemporary American Poetry and Prose* (New Rivers Press, Moorhead, MN). Other poems appeared in *The Northstone Review* (Minneapolis, MN).

*from* SKY THICK WITH FIREFLIES

"Third Elegy," *The Recorder* (New York, NY), "Nighttime on the Island," *Even the Daybreak: 35 Years of Salmon Poetry* (Salmon Poetry, Ireland), "Remembering Karen Ann Quinlan," *The Northstone Review* (Minneapolis, MN), "In My Father's Voice," *Open-Eyed, Full-Throated: An Anthology of American-Irish Poets* (Arlen House, Ireland), "Dear God of H_____," *The Heart of All That Is: Reflections on Home* (Holy! Cow Press, Duluth, MN). Other poems appeared in *Salmon: A Journal in Poetry 1981-2007*, Salmon Poetry (Ireland), and The St. Paul Almanac (St. Paul, MN).

SWIMMING WITH SHADOWS

"Thanks," *St. Paul Almanac* (St. Paul, MN) and *Midwest Review* (Madison, WI), "Leaving," Winner, Garrison Keillor Poetry Contest 2015 (St. Paul, MN), "Bob's Rooster," *Lief* (St. Paul, MN), "Storm, Lake Superior," *Poetry Ireland Review* (Dublin, Ireland), "The Way Back" and "Our Ancestral Ghosts," *Open-Eyed and Full-Throated: An Anthology of American-Irish Poets* (Arlen House, Ireland), and "Lake," *postcardsandpoemsandprose* (wordpress.com, online).

ETHNA McKIERNAN has been twice
awarded a Minnesota State Arts Board grant
in poetry. Her first book, *Caravan*, was
nominated for the Minnesota Book Award
and her work has been widely anthologized,
including in *The Notre Dame Book of Irish
American Poetry*, *33 Minnesota Poets*, and
more. McKiernan holds an MFA from
Warren Wilson Program for Writers. Her
fourth book, *Swimming With Shadows*, was
published by Salmon Poetry (Ireland) in 2019.
McKiernan works in Street Outreach for a
non-profit serving the Minneapolis homeless
population. In an earlier life, she was CEO of
Irish Books and Media, Inc., a school bus
driver, and a grape picker in France.

# salmonpoetry

Cliffs of Moher, County Clare, Ireland

"Like the sea-run Steelhead salmon that thrashes upstream to its spawning ground, then instead of dying, returns to the sea—Salmon Poetry Press brings precious cargo to both Ireland and America in the poetry it publishes, then carries that select work to its readership against incalculable odds."

TESS GALLAGHER

# The Salmon Bookshop
# & Literary Centre

Ennistymon, County Clare, Ireland

*The Irish Times*
35 Best Independent Bookshops